VICTORIA
The Insider's Guide

VICTORIA
The Insider's Guide

Robert Moyes

ORCA BOOK PUBLISHERS

To my mother, for a million meals and a million other things;
and to my father, who bought me a dictionary and a copy of
Fowler's *Modern English Usage* in grade nine.

Copyright © 1997 Robert Moyes

Canadian Cataloguing in Publication Data
Moyes, Robert, 1953 –
  Victoria

  Includes bibliographical references
  ISBN 1-55143-079-7

  1. Victoria (B.C.) – Guidebooks. I. Title.
  FC3846.18.M69 1997   917.11'28   C96-910826-5   F1089.5.V6M69 1997

Library of Congress Catalog Card Number: 97-65297

Cover design by Christine Toller
Front cover photograph by Jeff Barber/INFocus Photography
Printed and bound in Canada

Orca Book Publishers   **Orca Book Publishers**
PO Box 5626, Station B   PO Box 468
Victoria, BC V8R 6S4   Custer, WA 98240-0468
Canada   USA

99 98 97   5 4 3 2 1

TABLE OF CONTENTS

I am profoundly grateful to the many people who made contributions to this book, and am delighted that they were able to help me in alphabetical order. All my thanks to: Lynne Bain, Jon Barss, Aaron Boles, Ian Cochran, Grant Edmonds, Chris Gower, Adam Heffelfinger, Sylvia Imeson, Nancy Moyes, and Lloyd Rushton.

INTRODUCTION

This is a completely new edition of a guidebook that first came out in 1990. Although it is now conveniently downsized to fit in your pocket, its informational usefulness has, if anything, increased. Some specialty references and other clutter have been removed; what remains is everything that is essential to having a successful stay in this fine city. Through its candid appraisals of the restaurants, an objective ranking of our numerous tourist attractions, and information about which are the best shops (and best bargains), this guide offers an honest and detailed summary of all you'll need to know about both "tourist" Victoria and the real city that dwells behind that appealing facade.

Victoria, nestled jewel-like at the southern tip of Vancouver Island, offers a legion of transient pleasures to the visitor and more abiding satisfactions for permanent residents. Most immediately apparent is the superb setting. Bounded by water on three sides, with marine vistas that culminate in the snow-capped peaks of the Olympic Mountains across the Strait of Juan de Fuca, Victoria has grown up amidst a gently rolling landscape that never lacks for pastoral charm. With its balmy, Mediterranean climate, a pedestrian- oriented downtown whose nineteenth-century buildings are attractively built to a human scale, and a full range of sophisticated urban amenities, Victoria is the quintessential island retreat. The city can be a little bit smug, perhaps, but the locals are always eager to share their beautiful surroundings and easy-going lifestyle with tourists and recent arrivals alike.

Even though this "city of gardens" is also the provincial capital, it is only in the last two decades that Victoria has seriously begun to search for a cosmopolitan identity. Up until the end of the seventies we were content to promote our "Little Bit of Olde England" image: a mostly successful attempt to package the city as a historical British theme park. But at least we came by our pretensions honestly, and it makes for an intriguing story.

Victoria was settled in 1843, when the autocratic James Douglas chose it as the site for the coastal fur-trading headquarters of the Hudson's Bay Company. At the time, he declared: "The place appears to be a perfect Eden ... so different in its general aspect from the wooded region around that one may be pardoned for supposing it had been dropped from the clouds." The ramshackle frontier town grew up almost overnight during the gold rush of 1858. Victoria was a natural funnel through which poured 25,000 miners en route to the gold fields in the rugged Cariboo region of the British Columbia mainland. Those boom years of outfitting gold-seeking hopefuls enriched Victoria; the miners fared less well.

Yet for all the frontier roustabouts, Victoria never lacked for a gentry class. Hudson's Bay officials, Royal Navy officers, gentleman farmers and successful merchants made the circuit of elegant balls and fancy tea parties on the elaborately landscaped estates of Victoria's earliest plutocrats.

By the turn of the century, Victoria's population was 20,000. Now a city instead of just a frontier town, Victoria, with its naval base and two great harbours, seemed poised to become one of the great seaports in the Pacific Northwest. Indeed, the city had already produced its first great architect, Francis Rattenbury. After winning the design competition for the Legislative Buildings at age 25, Rattenbury went on to design several other downtown landmarks — including the Empress Hotel, the Crystal Garden and the Marine Terminal — that are literally synonymous with the Inner Harbour. But despite our increasing maturity, Victoria began to be assailed by financial and political setbacks; before long the city was easily surpassed by both Seattle and Vancouver, who went on to cosmopolitan greatness. Victoria was content to be a sleepy little capital city.

For most of this century, Victoria has been viewed as the last bastion of stately stodginess, a pretty little backwater that lured tourists with such descriptive promotional slogans as "Follow the Birds to Victoria" and "The Garden City." But it is, of course, the "Little Bit of Olde England" shtick that has long since given Victoria its dominant tourist image of double-decker buses and crumpet-munching tea grannies.

These are just clichés, of course — a fact readily apparent to anyone who has ever been to England. Due to the towering Rocky Mountains which separate British Columbia from the rest of Canada, a natural north-south trading axis developed early on with California. Victoria's history — and many of our period houses — very much suggest that we were more a little bit of New San Francisco than of Olde England.

And yet the English influence was certainly profound. Many of our original settlers felt very strong ties with England, and weak ones with Canada. These displaced Britons, many of them soldiers or merchants who had spent long years in India or the Orient, now sought to recreate the England of their memory in this new land on the west coast. The result, although very much idealized, nonetheless had an authentic British stamp. From the English laws that kept our frontier much tamer than the American West to the ongoing traditions of pub lunches, garden-like parks, and public buildings, Victoria has earned the right to sport its tweeds and handlebar moustaches.

And who can argue with the success of this experiment in transplanted Englishness? The Empress Hotel receives hundreds of requests annually for the correct way to brew and present tea. And one of the tourist agencies in town is still laughing about a woman who came in, pointed at the Parliament Buildings, and asked, "Is that where the Queen lives?"

For 50 years or more, Victoria has lived with these clichés, and quite unashamedly used them to attract tourists. But the city has outgrown all those frumpy old images, and developed a far more contemporary style. The growth explosion throughout the Pacific Northwest has washed over southern Vancouver Island, and Victoria has become notably more sophisticated.

It is now possible to enjoy a heady range of activities in and around Victoria. There are many fine restaurants, the majority of which are within a 15-minute walk of the Inner Harbour; shopping is diverse, intimate, yet international in scope; the recreational choices range from scuba to golf, from windsurfing to nature rambles in regional parks; the arts and culture have blossomed, with a national-calibre opera company, one of Canada's first Fringe Festivals, and a world-class museum to name only three highlights. And nightlife in the clubs, pubs, and cabarets means that the fun's only just starting as the sun goes down.

But despite its undeniable growth spurt and newish veneer of sophistication, Victoria happily remains as much a community as a metropolis. Better yet, for a city that has, for too long, been obsessed with its past, Victoria is realizing that quaintness and charm can coexist with a little energy and chutzpah.

And now that Victoria has finally admitted that the Queen doesn't *really* live here, it's likely that the city with the colourful past can expect an equally intriguing future.

GETTING AROUND

The easily spotted Tourism Victoria facility, housed in the art deco tower at the north end of the Inner Harbour opposite the Empress Hotel, is the first place to head in order to get oriented and get the most out of your stay. Tourism Victoria's focus is primarily on Victoria, and it can help you get a hotel room, book a Tally-Ho tour, organize a salmon-fishing charter, or find out where Roger's Chocolates is. (It also has some stuff on Vancouver Island, the Gulf Islands, and mainland B.C., and if it doesn't have what you want, staff will at least dig out a useful contact number.)

Aside from handing out reams of information on the town's important tourist attractions, they also accept bookings for all the hotels and bed & breakfast operations that list with them, while their ticket centre sells everything from air flights and theatre tickets to daily bus passes. (Note that Tourism Victoria is sponsored by about 700 tourist-oriented businesses, and its staff only promotes those particular operations. Fortunately, with but a few exceptions, all the businesses you'd want to hear about belong.) During a busy day in August, up to 4,000 people come traipsing through those glass doors.

In addition to the well-trained and helpful staff, Tourism Victoria has wall-to-wall brochures and visitor publications for browsers wanting to research their own fishing charter or plan a hunt for Georgian silver along Antique Row. And whatever you do, don't forget to grab a free map, which is keyed with all the most popular tourist destinations (the maps are widely distributed throughout those racks of brochures).

Tourism Victoria is open daily between 9 AM and 5 PM. The phone number for the Travel Infocentre is 382-2127 and the number for accommodation reservations is 953-2022.

Another very useful guide to the city is *Monday Magazine*,

a free weekly that is distributed all over the downtown area in yellow boxes. Although *Monday* offers a real flavour of the politics and lifestyle of Victoria, you'll be most interested in its comprehensive calendar listings, which cover everything from opera to rummage sales.

TRANSPORTATION

More than three million tourists a year visit Victoria ... and that, coupled with our internal growing pains, has resulted in increasing traffic congestion and a perpetual parking problem downtown. Yet by the same token, that small downtown core, with its distinct areas and profusion of shops and restaurants, is ideal to tour on foot: just grab a map, put on those Reeboks, and take your measure of this grand city at an ambler's pace. (Comprehensive listings of the city's shops, broken down by area, are located in this guide's **Shopping** section.)

CAR RENTALS

Sad to say, Victoria's drivers are not among the world's best. Speeding isn't that much of a problem, but instances of rudeness and just plain incompetence are on the rise. If you want to put on the mileage, in either your own car or a rental, a little defensive driving is well advised. (And please note that you are advised to phone for a taxi; they almost never respond to an on-street hail.) Following is a list of some of the larger rental agencies:

Avis
1001 Douglas Street   386-8468

Budget
757 Douglas Street   953-5300

Rent-a-Wreck
2634 Douglas Street   384-5343

Tilden
767 Douglas Street   386-1213

Even with numerous private lots and big parkades (Johnson and Blanshard, Lower Yates, View and Douglas, and Broughton at Broad), parking can be a problem downtown. The rates are some of the cheapest in Canada, but check the signs carefully when you're street parking: they *will* tow during rush hour, typically from 4 PM to 6 PM. The meters are in operation from 8 AM till 6 PM, excluding Sundays and holidays.

TOURS

Victoria tours range from double-decker buses and horse-drawn carriages to harbour cruises in cute little tugboats (please check **Sightseeing** for details).

PUBLIC TRANSPORTATION

Victoria's public transport system is clean, efficient, and friendly, and those big buses go in a 32-kilometre radius as far afield as Sidney and Sooke (but frequency isn't their strongest suit, with many routes having only hourly service). A single adult fare costs $1.50 for one zone, and $2.25 for two; but your best bet is to buy an all-day pass for $5. Pick one up in the Tourism Victoria tower in the Inner Harbour; and while you're there, get the indispensable — and free — "rider's guide," with all the routes and times (it costs a quarter on the bus). Its 190 buses run daily from 6 AM till midnight, and the principal departure points include the corner of Douglas and Belleville (near the Empress Hotel) and farther downtown at the corner of Yates and Douglas. For information, call 382-6161.

RESTAURANTS

Despite Victoria's obsessive need to be "more English than the English," one vital activity that has been thankfully spared the stern hand of Empire is cooking. The British passion for boiling food to death never caught on here; that culinary clemency, combined with diverse immigration, has turned Victoria into a diner's paradise. With nearly 700 restaurants to pick from, even the fussiest eaters should find their favourite food groups here, and cooked up by the appropriate ethnic chef. Whether your passion is truffle soup or tortiere, souvlaki or sushi, it's readily available — and at surprisingly low prices.

I have given brief reviews of more than 50 restaurants. These are the ones that I and my friends keep going back to, the restaurants that consistently leave the customer feeling happy. Maybe there's a bonus because the waiter does sly juggling tricks or the soup bowl keeps getting refilled, but the bottom line is good food at a fair price. The listings are presented alphabetically, in three groupings ranging from least to most expensive; there is a brief blurb on coffee bars at the end.

LEAST EXPENSIVE

Barb's Place
310 St. Lawrence Street   *384-6515*

In a city full of fish-and-chip parlours, it takes a lot to stand out. Barb's solution was to build a floating takeout place and moor it at picturesque Fisherman's Wharf in James Bay. They only use halibut; the hand-hewn chips are served up in cleverly folded newspaper pouches; and there are wharfside picnic tables from which to admire the fishing fleet, the more stationary fleet of funky houseboats … and the squawking gulls who wait patiently for a handout. (If you're not a fan of good and greasy fish and chips, they do equally tasty tricks with bacon burgers, "wharf dogs," and a very creamy clam chowder.)

Beacon Drive-In
126 Douglas Street 385-7521

Sited at the edge of Beacon Hill Park, the Beacon Drive-In serves one of the best "diner-style" breakfasts in the city. Even though it identifies its different offerings by number, the food is surprisingly good: the eggs are never greasy, the bacon is crisp, and those thick pancakes are a treat. During the summer, the outside tables are the best bet: you can watch joggers in the park, or feed crumbs to the tiny birds who might make a skittering landing at the edge of your table. The Beacon is a real hangout for the people in James Bay — everyone from senior citizens to single moms drops in for food and friendship.

Bohematea
515 Yates Street 383-2829

This self-styled "funky teahouse" is a classic hole-in-the-wall, with retro light fixtures and mismatched furniture straight from a yard sale. It also has dramatic brick walls, obliging staff, and the best vegetarian food in the city. The Sri Lankan chef follows Ayurvedic principles, and uses only fresh, high-quality ingredients. Lighter bites include soup, roti (no-yeast flatbread), and burritos made with refried beans and raw veggies that are served cold. Heartier eaters can choose among generously proportioned sandwiches (including a tasty sundried tomato and eggplant melt), a Lebanese pita bread roll, and Tuscan-style rotini. Some people swear they have the best pizza in the city (try the one with ginger pesto, Monterey jack, mushrooms, and olives); and a friend of mine who auditioned the place loved the food so much that he came back the next day for more. Their tea menu is exceptional: specialty teas (ginseng and ginger, cranberry and sage, peppermint brewed in hot chocolate), herbal infusions, and a wide selection of green, black, and flavoured teas. They also have exotic iced teas in summer.

Burrito Express
140-560 Johnson Street 381-2333

Handily situated in Old Town's Market Square, this hole-in-the-wall takeout parlour dishes up some pretty fine

Mexican fare at exceptionally low prices. The beef and bean
enchilada is big enough to guarantee sufficient energy for a
few more hours of power shopping (and if you ask for extra
hot sauce, make sure you've got an ice-cold Coke handy). For
about a dollar more, you can invest in the tasty taco salad.

C'est Bon
10 Bastion Square   *381-1461*

If you're looking for a light bite with some continental elegance,
here's the place. C'est Bon's on-site bakery supplies the basis
for various designer croissants (try either the ham and cheese
or the brie and herb); it also produces spicy focaccia bread,
which is used to make either meat or vegetarian deli sandwiches.
The soups are great here, as are all those sinfully tasty cookies.
Small and cheery, C'est Bon offers classical music, warm brick
walls, natural light and free newspapers to its sit-in patrons.
Those on the go can either take out items off the menu or maybe
grab a crusty baguette and have a harbourside picnic. It's also
good for breakfast: the continental features croissants and jam,
a fresh fruit salad, and that ever-essential caffeine beverage.

Demitasse Coffee Bar
1320 Blanshard Street   *386-4442*

If you like your bistros with an artsy/bohemian touch, there's
nothing better in Victoria than the Demitasse. An institution
since it opened in 1981, the Demi serves big mugs of the best
coffee in the city — both ordinary java and designer lattes and
mochas. The menu's star attraction is the "early bird," a croissant-
and-scrambled-egg plate that can be customized several ways
(try it with ham or the spicy Portuguese sausage). They also
have bagels, a filling bowl of fruit and yoghurt, thick sandwiches and a hearty borscht. The walls are covered with art,
the stereo plays Stan Getz or Scarlatti, and the service is friendly.

Dutch Bakery
718 Fort Street   *385-1012*

If an old-fashioned coffee shop holds any appeal, then don't
overlook this venerable Victoria institution. The Dutch Bakery
has been serving up hearty food for 40 years now, and the prices
seem to be about a decade behind the times. For breakfast,
aside from the regular stuff, consider tucking into a couple of

croquettes or else the *uitsmyter*, which is Dutch-style ham and
eggs. Come lunch, they serve various hot sandwiches (the burgers and the reuben are recommended), the soups are always
fine, the coffee's passable and the service is quick. An older
crowd comes here, and they fit right in with the pine walls
decorated with Delft china plates. And leave your diet at the
door ... at dessert time, those vanilla slices, dollar rolls, sacher
tortes, flying saucers, and chocolate eclairs taste even better
than they look.

Eugene's Greek Snack Bar
1280 Broad Street   *381-5456*

If you like Greek "fast food," then head over to Eugene's: this
self-serve restaurant may be the best meal deal in all Victoria.
They do a great donair (that vertical spit of hand-pressed meat
which is shaved off as needed), the lamb and pork souvlaki are
first-rate, and they serve up a generous plate of the tastiest squid
this side of Corfu. The spinach pie and the lentil soup are also
recommended. Many of the dishes can be ordered in combination with a fine Greek salad, and snackers can get by with an
order of pita bread and hummus or tzatziki. All the familiar
Greek wines are available by the glass or carafe.

Italian Foods Import
1114 Blanshard Street   *385-7923*

Want to have a picnic in the country? Then take your little
hamper down to Italian Foods Import and stock up! Start with
a crusty baguette fresh daily from the Italian Bakery, then maybe
ask for some Genoa salami, prosciutto or capicolli (deliciously
spiced hams). Your cheese plate could contain asiago, fontina,
gorgonzola, or French brie (and if you want *real* olives on the
side, they have tubs with several Greek and Italian varieties).
And no picnic is complete without treats; this deli stocks Baci
chocolates, amaretto-flavoured biscuits and rum crisps, and a
variety of Italian candies. There's also a small lunch bar where
you can order lasagna, soup, sandwiches and sausage rolls (and
gelati for dessert).

J & J Wonton Noodle House
1012 Fort Street   *383-0680*

With noodle-making machinery brought in especially from

Hong Kong and the chefs on display behind glass walls, it's no wonder that the crowds showed up when noted restaurateur Joseph Wong opened his latest venture. It's been more than a year now, and the crowds are still queuing for lunch: guess the best gimmick is still to have good food at reasonable prices. If you don't go for the lunch special, you can choose amongst noodles in soup, chow mein, and congee (rice broth). The hot and sour soup is tasty, and the egg rolls come with the plum sauce already tucked inside. There are some spicy selections, and Joseph is proud that they cook their own barbecued duck and pork from scratch (most other restaurants don't). Dinner isn't pricy, and ranges from curried duck to stir-fried beef with sweet-and-sour pineapple sauce. Although the food doesn't try to be gourmet and the decor hovers just a notch above functional, J & J offers a tasty experience that is unique amongst Victoria's many Chinese restaurants.

Sam's Deli
805 Government Street   382-8424

If a soup and sandwich place is what you're looking for, the ever-popular Sam's Deli will fill the bill — and your tummy — handsomely. Even the locals brave the noon-hour lineups to get their hands on those bulging sandwiches that the cheery counter folk dish up: the house classic is the towering shrimp and avocado, but Americans seem to go for the turkey (the roast beef is equally tasty). The homemade soups are excellent, as is the chili. The ambience indoors is fine, but the cafe tables offer great views of the harbour and the people scurrying by along Government Street. Or why not order your lunch as takeout, and head down to the wharf and catch a free show from the buskers?

The Sally
714 Cormorant Street   381-1431

An easy-going spirit of bohemianism pervades this fine restaurant: from the amply stocked reading rack to the Matisse-influenced hand-painted table tops, this is the perfect hideaway from the slick veneer that Victoria has acquired from years of selling itself to tourists. The mainstay of the restaurant is its foot-high sandwiches, which include several vegetarian options as well as a delicious curried chicken and apricot charmer or else a pastrami with lots of big-city swagger. Bagel melts, hearty soups, and several hefty salads (including Greek, Thai noodle, and spinach) round out the food offerings. There is also a full roster of designer coffees and carbonated beverages, and a dozen fancy teas that are blended locally. Stylishly funky, the Sally has lots of personality but no pretensions.

Wah Lai Yuen
560 Fisgard Street 381-5355

This clean and sparsely decorated restaurant is considered by many Chinese to be the "McDonald's of Chinatown" (but they're not being unkind!). The menu goes on for miles, but you can do very well on the first page, which lists all the soups. The won ton can be a bit bland; I'd recommend the noodle soup with barbecued pork and beef balls, which is filling and flavour-drenched. (The barbecued pork is excellent here, as are the rich and moist pork buns). Another classic is the steamed Chinese broccoli with oyster sauce. Service is fast and the food is among the cheapest in Chinatown. Give in to those beguiling smells from the bakery and buy a sticky bun to nibble on as you head out the door.

MODERATELY PRICED

Barkley's
777 Douglas Street 382-7111

With its tall windows, peach-coloured walls, and subtle floral carpeting, Barkley's is as elegant a restaurant as you'll find in Victoria. Although nobody says you have to wear a tie, you may feel under-dressed at noon if your ensemble doesn't boast at least a cellular phone: the business crowd comes here in force, and they are definitely *doing* lunch. Barkley's offers a full range of fine French cuisine: they have steak, seafood, chicken and pasta (if you can't settle on one entrée, be greedy and try the mixed meat grill). The seafood bisques are creamy and rich, while the Caesar salads are particularly regal. Service is exemplary and prices are more than fair.

The Blue Crab
146 Kingston Street 480-1999

Aptly enough for a harbourside restaurant, this understatedly elegant bar and grill puts an emphasis on seafood, with choices ranging from salmon, crab, tiger prawns, and clams to various seafood pastas. Lunch guests can choose from a broad menu: sandwiches (the Mediterranean chicken, served on focaccia, offers a medley of sunny and subtle flavours), salads, and pasta. Dinner options are a bit more exotic: if you don't fancy the locally raised emu, how about the New Zealand orange roughy or the mussels and house-smoked chicken sausage in a Portobello mushroom broth? Everything is made from scratch, on the premises; the chef incorporates various Asian influences, and puts together unusual combinations with notable flair. And if you get bored staring out those huge windows at the adjoining marina, check out the whimsical Klee-style plates. Service is deft and very obliging.

The Blue Fox
101-919 Fort Street   *380-1683*

Hearty food in a casual environment is what's for sale in this attractively unpretentious bistro. The breakfasts — including various versions of eggs Benedict, as well as huevos rancheros, three-egg omelettes, and killer french toast — are tasty indeed, and generously portioned. Lunch, which is always well subscribed by the Fox's many fans, includes burgers, sandwiches, quiche, and quesadillas. The place is small, which means that non-smokers can get a snootful of carcinogens if they are anywhere near the fire zone. Service is prompt, but you will have time to check out all the *Far Side* cartoons that are mounted underneath the Plexiglas tabletops.

Cafe Mexico
1425 Store Street   *386-1425*

With its wood plank floors, garlands of peppers and garlic, ceiling fans, plaster and brick walls, and Dos Equis posters, this place is an attractive pastiche of a Tex-Mex roadhouse. Although they serve all the classics, like enchiladas, chimichangas, tacos, and chile rellenos, this tasty cuisine definitely comes from Mexico via California. Yet if the food is a hybrid, the service is pure West Coast: cheerful, high-spirited, and young. If you're not up to a jug of margaritas or one of the half-dozen brands of Mexican beer they stock, try the cinnamon-flavoured coffee. Their dinner specials are a good bet. Sometimes they play tapes featuring the soulful music of local Latino Julio Cabrera.

Caffe Brio
944 Fort Street 383-0009

It's unusual to review a restaurant that's not even built yet, but when one of the city's best chefs is getting together with a gifted restaurateur and they have a great idea ... well, I wanted you to at least *know* about it. Sylvia Marcolini is from Tuscany, and she has always dreamed about promoting authentic regional Italian food in Victoria. In concert with head chef Sean Brennan they will marry traditional Tuscan cuisine with a "West Coast" sensibility. Expect affordable comfort food — simple, honest, and good and made from the freshest possible local ingredients. Just like in Italy, the menu will change with the seasons: more game in winter, lighter and more vegetarian in spring. As well as variations on classics such as osso buco and puttanesca, Caffe Brio will boast an antipasto bar and a walk-through garden. No guarantees, but this could be a classic! (Caffe Brio should be open just about when this book comes back from the printer.)

Camille's
45 Bastion Square 381-3433

If genuinely gourmet food at upper-moderate prices sounds tempting, then don't hesitate to visit this charming shrine to the gastronomic good life. Intimate and casually elegant, Camille's features "West Coast" cuisine: international influences combined with a fetish for local ingredients (for example, they grow their own herbs and bake their own bread). The bouillabaisse is spiced to perfection, the Caesar salad is fine, seafood bisques are richly flavoured, and their signature rack of lamb is truly memorable (especially if it's washed down with one of the innumerable Bordeaux stashed in the cellar). Host and chef David Mincey is one of Victoria's most knowledgeable wine experts: part of the decor consists of hundreds of empty bottles, whose labels function like wallpaper and bear testimony to this wine-lover's scholarship. David wears his expertise lightly, and can make useful suggestions for memorable wine and food pairings.

Wine expert David
Mincey of Camille's:
innovative West
Coast cuisine

La Cucina
920 Gordon Street   *381-4556*

If fine Italian food at fair prices is what's needed, then check out
this cosy downtown restaurant. The regular menu includes all
the standards like veal, lasagna, and eggplant parmigiana (the
dinner entrées typically come with veggies and a delicious side
serving of pasta that's subtly spiced with dill). People with smaller
appetites can choose from various pasta dishes, or just settle
for salad and the hearty minestrone soup, which is made daily.
The desserts are fine, particularly the bacio, a generous ball of
rich chocolate ice cream with a coffee liqueur centre and a shawl
of almond extract-flavoured whipping cream. For lunch you
might wish to ignore the menu and opt for the tasty smorgasbord.

Da Tandoor
1010 Fort Street   *384-6333*

There's little argument that this is the best East Indian restaurant in the city. The atmosphere, with its intricately carved sandalwood screens, tapestries, fabric paintings, and plangent sitar
music, stirs the senses almost as much as the spicy food aro-
mas in the air. The restaurant is named after the clay ovens
central to much Indian cooking. For starters, the mulligatawny
soup is fine. And order some "naan," the wonderful,
pancake-flat bread that is cooked briefly in the beehive-shaped

oven, then served with a dip (I'd recommend the spicy Egg-plant Bharta). For entrées they have several special platters that offer a banquet of tastes and flavours. I'd also recommend the Bhuna Gosht, lamb that's been cooked with fresh toma-toes, onions, ginger, and garlic. Da Tandoor also has a good range of seafood dishes, and their vegetarian plates are prized by many of my non-carnivorous friends. Lunch is also a good bet; many people go for the smorgasbord, but you can order off the menu. The service is deft and courteous here (and if you are used to hot food, their "hot" dishes shouldn't take your head off).

Dilettante's Cafe
787 Fort Street   *381-3327*

Ever since it opened in 1995 this intimate restaurant has had lineups at the door. Run by three women with impeccable culi-nary credentials, Dilettante's offers elegantly handmade food at surprisingly reasonable prices. The lunch menu includes a good mix of appetizers, sandwiches, burgers, and pasta items (the sandwich featuring roasted red pepper, eggplant, asiago, and pesto mayonnaise is a classic). Entrées come with a choice of salad or thick-cut french fries that verge on the addictive. At dinnertime, the menu expands to include such items as lamb (this special changes with the chef's mood and is always worth having), free-range chicken breast, polenta, and West Coast salmon. Lighter diners should consider the phyllo pie stuffed with goat's cheese and wild mushrooms or else the very fine spinach salad. The wine list is small but well chosen. Sunday brunch, notable for several versions of eggs Benedict, is also worth a try. There are only 14 tables so arrive early for lunch; reservations accepted at dinner.

Don Mee
538 Fisgard Street   *383-1032*

One of the oldest and best-known of Victoria's Chinese restau-rants, elegant Don Mee's continues to serve large portions of well-prepared, middle-of-the-road, Canadianized Chinese food. This is the favoured eating place of many of Victoria's Chinese-Canadians for business lunches and big social occa-sions. The dim sum is the best in town: the metal carts and large bamboo steaming baskets offer up as many as 50 gourmet goodies, everything from shrimp in fancy pastry wrappings to fried jellyfish in ginger sauce or that old standby, chicken's feet. The less adventurous can sample the rice and fried noodle dishes, the almond boneless chicken, or the special combo plate. At dinner, instead of chow mein, fried prawns, chop suey, etc., you might consider such house specialties as pork cutlets sautéed with coffee sauce, or fresh oysters either in a hot pot or pan-fried with ginger and onion.

Herald Street Caffe
546 Herald Street   *381-1441*

Right when it first opened in 1982, Herald Street Caffe was a sell-out success … and those lineups have never gone away. Friendly yet a notch upscale, here's a restaurant that has taken a core of Italian cuisine and applied lots of West Coast moxie. Appetizers include yellowfin tuna carpaccio and a delicious baked brie, which comes complemented by chutney (use the deliciously heavy white bread to mop up any stray rivulets of cheese). Their pasta is made fresh daily and comes dressed for dinner in nine different outfits, including a hearty cannelloni and a tasty combination of creamed gorgonzola, romano, and parmigiano with green peas. Their bamboo "steamer" can be ordered vegetarian or with fish. Come dessert time, try the incomparable Shaker lemon pie. They have an award-winning wine cellar, and many of their wines are sold by the glass. Although originally an evenings-only place, Herald Street opened for the lunch trade in 1989 and proved an immediate hit. And no restaurant in town can rival the beauty and extravagance of their floral displays.

Hunan Village
546 Fisgard Street   *382-0661*

If you like your Chinese food hot, but don't know how to pronounce "Szechuan," pay a visit to Hunan Village. Run by the three Yang brothers, the Hunan insists on using only first-class ingredients … and there's no MSG on the premises. Start with a bowl of their hot and sour soup (and if it's summertime, consider following it with the cold eggplant salad, which is a marvellous and unusual dish). Anything they do to seafood or chicken is worth a try; my favourites are Hunan shrimp and hot and sour chicken. (If the fiery cuisine of this mountainous

Chinese province is too robust, they also serve some Cantonese dishes.) The Hunan also puts on a fine — and inexpensive — lunch; the various rice or noodle plates are your best bet.

Il Terrazzo
555 Johnson Street   *361-0028*

If thoughts of genuine Italian cooking make you cry out *mama mia*, then hurry to this elegant charmer, which combines Tuscan cuisine with tasty touches of the West Coast. The restaurant proper boasts brick archways and colourful artwork, but most people are drawn to the eponymous terrace, where vines, riots of fuschia, old-fashioned strawberry pots, and brick fireplaces create a deliciously relaxed mood. (Unobtrusive natural gas heaters take up the slack on those days when the weather is sullen.) Lunch ranges from designer pizza, pasta dishes, and numerous salads to more elaborate offerings of fish and chicken (which can come with exotic combinations such as mango, asparagus, banana pepper, and basil). They also feature *tramezzino*, a sandwich made from focaccia bread. The dinner menu is more ambitious: aside from standard fare such as cannelloni and veal there are less common offerings such as carpaccio (sliced raw beef tenderloin with parmesan). The wood-oven-baked rack of lamb is a good bet, and a stand-out appetizer is the bruschetta and baked garlic bulb.

James Bay Tearoom
332 Menzies Street   *382-8282*

Despite the many cruel jibes hurled at English cuisine, the food at this tearoom/restaurant is fine indeed. The walls are covered with photos of England and the Royal Family and the service is deft and genuinely friendly — just the spot for breakfast and a perusal of the morning paper! Their omelettes and other egg dishes are tasty, and they come with hash browns and your choice of toast, scones, or muffins to tantalize your stiff upper lip. The coffee is good and your cup gets refilled just before you're about to ask. Lunch ranges from hamburgers, sandwiches, and salads to such redoubtable British fare as steak and kidney pie and Cornish pasties. Dinners include roast beef with Yorkshire pudding, liver and onions, quiche lorraine, chicken, and trout.

Japanese Village
734 Broughton Street   *382-5165*

Here's my favourite Japanese restaurant, and the only one in
Victoria where the food is cooked at small U-shaped tables
right in front of you, teppan-style (great for larger parties). So
what if all that razzle-dazzle stuff where the chef twirls his
knife and bangs out a backbeat on the salt and pepper shakers
is a tad corny — the food here is super. The steak, particularly
the filet mignon, is superbly tender; the seafood is delicate and
fresh. Their sauces, including a sweet ginger potion for chicken
and seafood, will have you eyeing that rapidly emptying plate
with dismay. Unlike the more contemporary look at other Japanese restaurants, the Village is dimly lit, with a sense of feudal
formality created by dark wood, rice-paper screens, and some
artfully arrayed warrior gear, which looks like it came from a
Kurosawa film: what better setting could there be for a
chef-as-samurai? They serve a great lunch from Monday to
Friday (try the steak and chicken teriyaki combo), but you only
get the full show if you turn up at dinnertime.

Jimmy's Place
1951 Oak Bay Avenue   *595-1112*

If you've spent the day behind Oak Bay's "tweed curtain" and
need to eat before heading back downtown, you can drop into
Jimmy's Place with complete confidence … as long as there's
room for you. Deservedly popular, this modestly priced restaurant serves continental cuisine with an Italian accent. Their
pasta specials are always reliable, the Greek and Caesar salads
are super, and the charbroiled lemon chicken is tender and delicious. They also serve up one of the best pizzas in the city.
Friendly and elegant — there is real linen on the tables and
service to match — Jimmy's is fine for lunch or dinner.

Kaz
100–1619 Store Street   *386-9121*

This popular, unpretentious restaurant handily dispels the no-
tion that "eating Japanese" means an empty wallet and a half-
full stomach. There are more than 30 items on the sushi menu,
which includes *temaki* (those attractive cone-shaped rolls). Both
lunch and dinner offer a full range of chicken and seafood items,
either teriyaki or karaage (deep-fried). If you're not a connois-

seur of sea urchin sushi, then maybe play it safe and go for one of the bento boxes for lunch: for an extra couple of dollars you can add on your choice of two extras such as chicken teriyaki or tempura vegetables (which are delicately battered here). Sited at the edge of Old Town just by the harbour, Kaz has just enough rice paper and blond wood to create a Japanese mood without going overboard. Service is prompt and friendly.

Koto's
510 Fort Street   382-1514

With colourful atmosphere, sit-down booths, and tasty food, Koto's has been offering Victorians a little taste of Tokyo for more than a decade. The lunch menu features O-bento, those partitioned lacquer boxes that come with a selection of teriyaki beef and chicken, tempura vegetables, or breaded salmon. They also offer the hard-to-find Ramen soup — hot noodles in chicken broth with sliced pork, bean sprouts, corn, and green onions. Up at the sushi bar, the bandanna-sporting chef dishes up the obligatory selection of sushi and sashimi. The dinner menu is more elaborate; try the teriyaki salmon or, if you're feeling posh, go for the elaborate seafood plate, featuring Alaskan king crab, salmon and geoduck. There's a good wine selection, and they even have cheesecake for dessert instead of just the ubiquitous vanilla ice cream.

Milestones
812 Wharf Street   381-2244

Despite having a hammerlock on the walk-by tourist trade thanks to their killer location at the north edge of the Inner Harbour, Milestones goes out of its way to serve tasty food at surprisingly reasonable prices — no wonder it's always busy. The breakfast and lunch menu offers a wide range of surprisingly trendy choices: baked goat cheese and roasted garlic or chipotle pesto potatoes for appies, maybe followed by a Portobello mushroom sandwich. The grilled chicken focaccia sandwich, which is dressed with smoked mozzarella and pesto mayonnaise, is a treat. There are pasta and burger offerings for the more conventionally minded. Their "specialty brunches" are notable, too. Dinner favours chicken, pasta, and seafood platters plus a wide range of steaks and ribs. If you get thirsty, there is micro-brewed beer on tap, plus a wide selection of designer martinis. With those harbour views, an obliging staff, and generous portions, it's hard to fault the place (well, the coffee *is* weak and the Caesar salads are certainly on the bland side). Otherwise, though....

Millos
716 Burdett Street   382-4422

If you want to be reminded of that idyllic vacation you had on Mykonos a few years back, revive your memories of those Mediterranean pleasures in this upscale taverna — just look for the building with the windmill, a block east of the Conference Centre. Although the menu makes a few concessions to western palates (including steaks and chicken cordon bleu), why not follow Zorba's example and go for the gusto? If baby squid are too scary, there're always those bacon-wrapped prawns or a selection of souvlaki (aside from lamb and beef they also have halibut). Light eaters can get by with a few selections from the appetizer section; heartier appetites might want the classic moussaka or else the wonderful rack of lamb. Millos is often packed, and deservedly so. There are three dining areas, funky murals, an attractive jungle of plants, and just enough Aegean blue and white decorative motifs so you get the idea. On the weekends, spirited dancers supply some extra passion and sparkle.

The Old Vic
1316 Broad Street   383-4536

To say that the Old Vic offers the city's best fish and chips is a woeful understatement: an English bloke I know who just happens to be a food writer claims that they serve the best he's ever tasted anywhere in Canada. The Old Vic is in its umpteenth incarnation as a fish and chip joint: the vintage highback wood booths are turn-of-the-century and the brass-accented decor is pure sixties. The menu is limited to three types of white fish, prawns, oysters, scallops, and side-order standards like onion rings and chowder. And they also have that indispensable British classic, mushy peas. Current owner Dick Wass, a reformed Yorkshireman who set up shop here in 1995, uses four different suppliers so that he can offer the freshest possible fish; he also makes sure that those crisp fries are homemade. If you want some authentic English nostalgia

— and some excellent, unrepentantly deep-fried food — then you can't do better than here.

Pagliacci's
1011 Broad Street   386-1662

In 1979, restaurateur-to-be Howie Siegel went looking for an espresso … and couldn't find one. What he *did* find was the resolve to quit his day job and open a hip, downtown bistro. Pagliacci's was an instant hit, and its cheekily pun-filled menu has been offering variations on the theme of Italian soul food to thousands of enthusiastic Victorians ever since. Howie "works the room" better than anyone in the city, and everyone is made to feel like family — just as well, considering how close together those tables are jammed. The place is always crowded, so come at off-hours for lunch and be prepared to stand in line if you simply *must* have veal medallions or the tortellini for dinner. There are 19 à la carte pastas to choose from, and they come in two sizes. The food is all made by hand, so grab a litre of wine, munch on the steaming focaccia bread, and eavesdrop on your neighbours while you're waiting. Howie also doubles as one of Victoria's most successful impresarios, and, *except* on weekends, there's always a jazz quartet, an R&B ensemble or some klezmer (gypsy jazz) music to keep the joint packed till the wee hours every night. They also do a nice Sunday brunch, starting at 11 AM.

Pescatore's
614 Humboldt Street   385-4512

Victoria is surprisingly short on seafood restaurants, but here's a good one … and just within casting length of the Inner Harbour. Plush and elegant, with grandly high ceilings, lots of plant life, and striking art by gifted local painter Luis Merino, Pescatore's is upmarket but affordable. The lunch specials are worth a look, but you may not get any further than the well-stocked oyster bar. Aside from various seafood items such as crab cakes and tiger prawns, they serve a wide range of pastas and bistro sandwiches. Their seafood bisques are lushly creamy. At dinner the menu expands to include trout, scallops, and rack of lamb for the serious carnivore; the appetizer list also changes to include carpaccio as well as smoked salmon with bocconcini. Their well-chosen wine list has convenient categories such as "reds for fish" and "big reds." Service is deft here and the food definitely merits a better-to-best designation.

Re-bar
50 Bastion Square   361-9223

Re-bar is welcome news to both vegetarians and anyone else who prizes fresh, wholesome food prepared with real affection. It started life as a juice bar, and liquid lunchers can still choose from 80 different fruit and vegetable potions, which can then be accessorized with anything from ginseng and bee pollen to ginger and blue-green algae. But the menu has long since expanded to include more substantial fare, with Asian and Italian influences strongly apparent. Re-bar's innovative chefs promote what they call "Modern Food," with the emphasis on less processed ingredients and on creating interesting new combinations: a tortilla, for example, that has an Oriental-accented filling. Vegetarian beginners may want to start with something like the best-selling almond burger; more adventurous choices are always available, and vegans and lactose-intolerant diners can dine here happily. This style of cooking is very hands-on — there is a lot of chopping and other preparation — but the wait is certainly worth it.

Rebecca's Food Bar
1127 Wharf Street   380-6999

If you want to combine the old and the new, pull up a chair at this elegant eatery, which is sited in a waterfront heritage building yet offers some of the city's most interesting and some-times adventurous cuisine. Cathedral windows look out over the Inner Harbour, but don't get so distracted by the view that you forget to peruse the menu! Lunches feature pasta, hip variations on the sandwich theme, and other goodies such as mussels, spanakopita, and a great moussaka. The "daily specials" sheet varies all the time and typically offers interesting ingredients in exciting combinations. Even the selection of warm breads — a basket typically includes focaccia, plain, and hot pepper — shows thought and verve. Come the dinner hour, venison, duck, unusual pasta combinations and several tasty salads get added to the menu. Sweet-toothed gluttons can finish off by choosing any three of the memorable homemade desserts via the generously portioned "sampler plate." Opened in 1990, Rebecca's quickly established a reputation for its imaginative treatment and presentation of West Coast cuisine.

San Remo
2709 Quadra Street   384-5255

Although Greek purists might raise an eyebrow, it's not by chance that out-of-the-way San Remo always has lineups at dinnertime. Prices are fair, service is fast and friendly, and the food is some of the best in town. Menu highlights include garlic prawns, charbroiled chicken breasts, and a lasagna that has a slight flavour of moussaka about it. All the standard Mediterranean munchies such as squid, hummus, souvlaki, and pita bread are here, plus more unusual treats like saganaki — goat's cheese flambéed with brandy and lemon. Light biters might want just the cheese pie and salad; those who want it all should order the weighty Platter for Two. They also dish up excellent pizza.

Santiago's
660 Oswego Street   388-7376

Now that tapas — most typically Spanish appetizers — have become trendy, too many restaurants are dishing up snappy little snacks with inflated prices. If you want to revel in the real thing, then visit Santiago's, which offers a wide range of tapas from Spain and various South American countries (but there are salads, burgers, and pizza for customers unprepared for voluptuously spicy food). Friendly and informal, Santiago's is done up in tropical colours with Latin decorative accents that range from elegant tapestries to salt and pepper shakers rendered as miniature bottles of Corona. The signature dish is the antipasto plate, a near-meal for two that includes baked garlic, ceviche, marinated veggies, Mediterranean olives, eggplant hummus, exotic salad greens, and a crusty baguette with garlic butter. Just a few of the other notable menu choices include the empañadas and the exotic papas arequipeña (Peruvian potatoes spiced with onion, peanuts, crushed chilies, cream, and feta). They do a nice breakfast, and the weekly specials are also worth a look. There's a small but well-chosen wine list, and a tasty batch of sangria is always waiting to be poured. Santiago's is worth a visit just for its festive atmosphere, but it also offers some of the best, most interesting food in all Victoria.

Szechuan Restaurant
853 Caledonia Avenue   384-0224

The decor in this Chinese restaurant may be plain and unpretentious, but the food is hot, spicy, and delicious. The menu is
wide-ranging, the prices low, and the familiar offerings such
as egg rolls and lean pork coexist with a number of zingy treats
for the palate: Hot and Sour Soup, Eight Treasure Chicken and
Jumbo Shrimps with Hot Bean Sauce are all good examples of
the incendiary cuisine of this mountainous Chinese province.
Although the truly adventurous might want to consider Strange
Taste Chicken or the Gourmet Jelly Fish, there is lots on the
menu for patrons who lack asbestos coatings on their tongues
(the menu clearly indicates which dishes will put your tem-
perature up a few degrees).

Taj Mahal
679 Herald Street   383-4662

Fans of East Indian cuisine will find that the Taj Mahal presents
the food of the Moghuls with taste and elegance — which is
only proper, considering that this self-confident restaurant is
built as a replica of its famed namesake. At lunchtime, the
daal soup, a snack platter of beef or veggie samosas, or the
kebabs will warm up a light eater. Diners looking for heartier
fare should consider choosing from the daily curry specials (if
you're used to hot food, then ask for *at least* a medium curry).
At dinnertime, there is a good selection of seafood and vegetarian dishes. Their three-course specials include papadams
(crisp, spicy wafers), appetizers such as pakora and kebabs,
and various entrées. The house special is the lamb or chicken
biryani, a celebratory dish fit for a prince.

Thai Siam
512 Fort Street   383-9911

Welcome to Victoria's most successful Thai restaurant, which
is a great place to savour how Thai chefs can take ordinary
ingredients such as ginger, mint, chilies, and curry, add more
exotic items such as lemon grass and lime leaves, and produce
a wonderful cuisine that is unique to all Asia. With its blond
wood, brick walls, and wicker chairs, Thai Siam creates a light
and airy mood. The lunch specials are worth considering; dinner patrons will have a much harder choice, as the 50-item

menu boasts an equal mix of seafood, meat, and vegetarian dishes, along with six memorable soups (I'm partial to #23 and #33, which star prawns, minced chicken, and a wide variety of spices). Some like it hot, but only long-time fans should ask for anything other than "medium" when ordering here. There is an extensive beer menu to put out any fires.

Tomoe
726 Johnson Street   *381-0223*

Although none of the restaurants in Victoria really seems to capture the ambience of a Tokyo eatery (and maybe that's a good thing), Tomoe is particularly authentic in its attention to the aesthetics of food presentation. With ritual and flair, the servers present a wide array of traditional Japanese dishes, including chicken, salmon, or beef teriyaki, sunomono or miso soup, seafood tempura, and, for the brave of stomach, sashimi (cuts of raw fish). Tomoe is handsomely done up in blond wood, translucent screens, and colourful banners; aside from regular open seating, it has a sequence of private tatami rooms and a sushi bar where the chef prepares two dozen examples of that finger-food-as-art. Aside from à la carte, there's a gourmet special every night, and a choice of four different fancy dinners for two or more (try the Shogun Dinner, which has a little bit of everything, including sushi, a lightly spiced chicken karaage, and whole crab's legs). Lunch is a busy time for this friendly and deservedly popular restaurant, with many coming for those clever bento box lunches.

The Wharfside
1208 Wharf Street   *360-1808*

Sited in a harbourside heritage building, the Wharfside is a warmly attractive study in brick, blond wood, and tile. There is a wraparound terrace with great water views, and the choice of indoor and outdoor seating. There is considerably more choice offered by the menu, whose several pages offer 11 burgers, a variety of seafood and pasta options, numerous sandwiches, and a dozen designer pizzas that are cooked in a wood-fired oven. They also offer a "light lunch" option for diners whose arteries are starting to get clogged after too many rich meals on the road. The fare is middle of the road, but done awfully well and benefiting from a few artful touches (such as

a medley of non-lettuce greens in the salad). Service is quick
and helpful; this is a good bet for families.

Yoshi Sushi
#601-771 Vernon Avenue   383-6900

Even though it's a bit of a drive away from downtown, Yoshi
Sushi is regularly packed with a lot of business types who ap-
preciate both the finely prepared and presented food and the
upscale decor. A loud "hello" will greet you from whichever
chef is tending the sushi bar next to the door. (Those seeking
privacy can be seated in the tatami rooms.) The menu ranges
from à la carte offerings such as deep-fried squid and various
noodle dishes to fancy dinners for two. Yoshi is the only restaurant in town with a "robata bar," which produces tender and
tasty shish kebabs (the chicken is super). The service isn't particularly attentive, but with a few gulps of sake you won't even
notice!

MORE EXPENSIVE

Chez Daniel
2524 Estevan Avenue   592-7424

If you love superb French cuisine, then pay your respects to
this small, fastidious restaurant: it's the best in the city. Daniel
Rigolet is an artist with a saucepan, and his dinners are *always*
inspired (you won't find salt and pepper shakers on the table!).
The Chateaubriand is exquisitely tender, the lamb and rabbit
dishes are elegant, and there's a small but well-chosen selection of seafood. Rigolet has also won many prizes for his wine
cellar, which can tantalize even jaded oenophiles. From the
scallops-in-saffron appetizer to raspberry sorbet for dessert, the
attention to flavour, texture, and presentation at Chez Daniel is
faultless. Not too pricey (and an absolute bargain given the
quality), no real food lover should pass this one up.

Deep Cove Chalet
11190 Chalet Road (near Sidney)   656-3541

"Life is nasty, brutish and short … make the most of it." This is
the kind of advice proprietor and chef Pierre Koffel is prone to
offer in his ads for the Chalet, which fluctuates between being
a fine restaurant to perhaps the finest on Vancouver Island.

Daniel Rigolet, of
Chez Daniel:
Victoria's finest chef

And if you agree with Koffel that life should be made the most
of, then maybe you owe yourself a visit to this handsome es-
tablishment, located waterside on manicured lawns about a
half-hour drive from downtown Victoria. Koffel is a supremely
gifted chef, lively and eccentric, who is either busy in the kitchen
whipping up delicious creations, bustling about serving wine,
or chatting up the regular customers, some of whom fly in from
Vancouver to spend $100 or more per head (or mouth) for the
splendiferous caviar and lobster spread, unless they've nosed
out the truffle soup at $38 a bowl. This artist has a superb touch
with traditional and not-so-traditional French cuisine, especially
seafood (always fresh and local), chicken, duck, beef, patés,
and vegetables. Desserts, too, are delightful: the homemade
sorbets are tart and refreshing (grab the raspberry if it's available), while the cheese plate is a grand way to pump up that
cholesterol level. The service can be slow and a shade offhand
on a busy Saturday night when the house is full of tourists. But
even then, the trek out to the Chalet is usually well worth the
effort … and the expense.

Empress Hotel Dining Room
721 Government Street   *389-2727*

The exquisitely formal dining room at the Empress Hotel has
the distinction of being the most expensive restaurant in all
Victoria. It's also one of the two finest. Head chef Iain Rennie
combines perfect formal training with great visual flair and a

Dining at the Empress Hotel: superb cuisine in the height of elegance

knack for unusual food combinations (such as adding a touch of candied lemon rind to the smoked salmon). The cream of mussel soup with walnuts is inspired, as is the breast of duck, which is lean and dark. The loin of lamb is, simply, superb. The dishes here are sophisticated, yet with a bit of a nod towards comfort food. The award-winning wine cellar is stocked with appropriate grandness, and the more than 300 choices draw mostly from California and the Pacific Northwest (and should you be celebrating, say, a fiftieth wedding anniversary, they will employ a sabre to open that bottle of Dom). The two-tiered mahogany dessert trolley seems like the height of wickedness ... until they trundle up later with all the cognacs, armagnacs, ports, and single malts. The room itself, which benefited from the Empress Hotel's $45-million renovation in 1989, is a stunning tribute to Edwardian elegance. The service, too, is polished, poised, and utterly beyond reproach. If your budget can handle entrées in the $30-$35 range, then an evening at the Empress is guaranteed to be magic.

The Marina Restaurant
1327 Beach Drive   *598-8555*

This is easily one of the most handsome restaurants in the city — and that's not even taking into account the million-dollar water views over the Strait of Juan de Fuca. Some regulars come here just for the sushi bar, but ignoring the menu would be a mistake: at 15 pages it offers everything from Szechuan salmon and the seafood hot pot to mango chicken and rack of lamb. The award-winning wine list features a Pacific Northwest theme, along with many Californian offerings (to say nothing of the 25 ports and dessert wines). Food quality has been known to vary here, and they've had to trim some of the trendier items in order to cultivate regular attendance by the culinary conservatives in nearby Oak Bay. But ever since it opened in 1994 the Marina has, with jaunty confidence, asserted itself as a landmark on the local food scene. Located just 10 minutes from downtown.

Sooke Harbour House
1528 Whiffen Spit Road   *642-3421*

A lot of people — including food critics from San Francisco, Toronto, and New York — consider Sooke Harbour House one of the best restaurants in the entire country, and it regularly makes it onto various Canadian "top ten" lists. This exquisite country inn is situated near the water about an hour's drive out of Victoria, and it's run with panache and passion by owners Sinclair and Frederica Philip. The cuisine isn't trendy ... it's trend-setting, with the emphasis on the freshest possible local ingredients, brought together in fresh ways. Sinclair regularly dons his scuba gear to bring such famous Sooke goodies as octopus, sea urchins, periwinkles, and whelks to the table; and the dinners are not only seasoned with herbs grown in the adjoining garden, but those flowers you thought looked so pretty could well end up as an inspired bit of colour and texture in a pasta salad. If you fancy salmon with rhubarb sauce or local veal sauced with thyme and tarragon, then head this way. Justly prized for its daring and dazzling cuisine, Sooke Harbour House is absolutely worth an overnight visit ... assuming you're lucky enough to get reservations. The rooms here, all with sea views and many with hot tub-equipped balconies, are gorgeously appointed with pottery, tapestries, carvings, and tilework from the area's best artists; as with the food, so too the hotel itself is a uniquely indigenous celebration of all that's best in this corner of the West Coast.

La Ville d'Is
26 Bastion Square   *388-9414*

If you love French cooking, but shy away from all those
heart-attack sauces, then try this elegant restaurant. Since the
late 1970s, Michel and Francoise Duteau have been sharing
the tasty cuisine of their native coastal Brittany with Victorians. Although this is a popular lunch spot, it's worth considering for that special night out. The food is prepared with concern
for both taste and texture, while the presentation is classically
elegant: exactly what you'd expect from one of the city's best
restaurants. The monkfish comes in a lightly spiced tomato
sauce, while the coquilles St. Jacques is simmered with a few
splashes of wine. (Aside from all the marine life, there are rabbit, rack of lamb, and beef tenderloin to assuage the pangs of
serious carnivores.) Michel is a truly charming host, convivial
and attentive. When complimented on a grandly satisfying entrée or the homemade kiwi ice cream, he is apt to shrug and
insist that "I got lucky." The wine list is small but effective,
with most of the bottles coming from France and California.

Vinsanto Urban Bistro
620 Trounce Alley   *480-0505*

At press time this upscale eatery was undergoing a makeover
from one of Victoria's best chefs, but it has always been a favourite with many of Victoria's more trendy diners. With its
high ceilings, elegant mill work, and tiled floor, Vinsanto makes
a dapper backdrop to a fancy night out on the town. It has a
short list of classic dinner entrees, including oven-roasted halibut, steak, and free-range chicken breast; and you may want to
start things off with the cornmeal-crusted oysters. Vinsanto also
boasts an extensive wine list. The open kitchen means that you
can watch as they cook your bow-tie pasta, and it's likely you
could learn a few tricks, as the food here is decidedly artful.
Bold combinations of ingredients and spices are common, and
even standard dishes can seem extra vivid. Coffee is exceptionally good and the service is fine. Lunch patrons, who can
choose from designer pizza, burgers, and sandwiches, may find
that the food is delicious — and resent that it only comes in
appetizer-sized portions.

COFFEE BARS

The Pacific Northwest is undoubtedly the coffee capital of North America, and Victoria has more than its share of trendy little enclaves awash in skinny lattes and frappuccinos. My favourite bean bistros include: **Torrefazione** (1230 Government Street, 920-7203), which is as Italian as its name, right down to its artfully hand-painted cups; the inescapable **Starbucks** (corner of Fort and Blanshard Street, 383-6208); and **Bogart's** (783 Fort Street, 383-7997), which serves a tasty brew and boasts an amiably classy owner.

SIGHTSEEING

Victoria's sights fall fairly neatly into two main groups: commercial attractions and museums. As the latter are all at least subsidized — and often run — by some level of government, it's a simple economic fact that they will generally offer better value for your sightseeing dollar. While the top commercial attractions are fine indeed, you may get the feeling that some of the lesser ones exist mainly as a gateway to the gift shop.

The sights are listed in categories, and in decreasing order of merit. The rankings are subjective and include the overall quality of the attraction and such related considerations as price, travel time, and scenery at the site and along the way.

Operating hours are listed, but not every seasonal fluctuation has been included. It's always best to call and check.

ATTRACTIONS

The Butchart Gardens
800 Benvenuto Drive   *652-5256*

What a joy to encounter an attraction that genuinely merits the over-used term "world class." A family operation for three generations, the Butchart Gardens has the taste and resources to do everything to perfection. In the "city of gardens," *this* is the one to see.

These 20 Eden-like hectares had their beginnings in 1904 when Jenny Butchart, the wife of a cement manufacturer, resolved to beautify an abandoned limestone quarry behind the family home at Tod Inlet on the Saanich Peninsula. She was a woman of tremendous energy — during the initial construction she even had herself lowered over the quarry cliffs in a bosun's chair to stuff ivy cuttings into any available crevice. Today, the Sunken Garden, with its rich palette of flowers and

The Japanese Gardens, Butchart Gardens
(*photo courtesy The Butchart Gardens Ltd.*)

graceful, curving paths, has become as much a Victoria icon as the Empress Hotel or the Parliament Buildings.

The Rose Garden, at its best in July, delights the senses of sight and smell with its hundreds of varieties, all carefully labelled. And each year the best new prize-winners join the old favourites. The exquisite, tree-shaded Japanese Garden, appropriately serene, provides an oasis of delicate green foliage. The symmetrical Italian Garden, with its lily-dotted reflecting pool, brings you back to the entrance.

But wait. No visit is complete without a second tour by night. From June to September, thousands of subtly placed lights transform the entire garden into a nocturnal wonderland quite different from its daytime counterpart. Trees seem to glow from within, and spotlights create a striking floral chiaroscuro. Most breathtaking of all is the celebrated Ross Fountain, whose endlessly changing sequence of water jets and lights produces a hypnotically beautiful effect.

To help bridge the gap between day and night tours, the Gardens, in July and August, mounts a glitzy, crackerjack musical revue, *Just For Fun*, on an outdoor stage. But the razzle-dazzle on stage is just a warmup for the *real* show, every Saturday night, when the Gardens shoots off about $20,000 worth of sensational fireworks. Set to a backdrop of light classical music, the fireworks — many of which are mounted on moving forms — are renowned for their artful whimsy: champagne bottles pop their corks and send out a literal shower of stars, an incandescent waterfall appears, and innocent butterflies cavort while volleys of more conventional roman candles light up the skies with their colourful cannonades. (To make the most of the fireworks, maybe come out to the Gardens around 5 PM, have dinner — their restaurant is excellent, but they provide lots of picnic tables as well — then tour the gardens till twilight. And after the show, it's time to take an unforgettable night-time stroll.)

Butchart Gardens is not just the best attraction in Victoria; it is considered the best in the entire province. More than 750,000 visitors come here annually — don't you miss it. Access is via the Pat Bay Highway; turn left at Keating Cross Road, and go straight for several kilometres. Open daily from 9 AM. Closing times fluctuate seasonally.

Crystal Garden
713 Douglas Street   *381-1213*

Once the largest saltwater swimming pool in the British empire — Johnny "Tarzan" Weissmuller set a world record here in the twenties — and much loved for its palm court teas and dances, this unique glass-topped building was reborn in 1980 as a tropical garden and aviary.

Visitors strolling among the ferns and hibiscuses may suddenly find themselves nose to beak with a Technicolor parrot or macaw. And one end of the conservatory houses a small zoo, where even more exotic creatures reside. Toucans, ibises, wallabies, lemurs, bats, and a family of pygmy marmosets (the world's smallest monkeys) are just a few of the denizens.

As the Crystal Garden is run by the Provincial Capital Commission, a branch of the B.C. government, signage and maintenance are of a high standard. A fine tea is served daily on the surrounding terrace. A family day pass is $20. July and August hours are 8:30 AM – 8 PM; winter hours are 10 AM – 4:30 PM.

Anne Hathaway's Cottage
429 Lampson Street   *388-4353*

In a city bursting with Victoriana, here's an attraction devoted to the era of an earlier queen — Elizabeth the First. Anne Hathaway's Cottage is a full-size replica of the thatch-roofed, half-timbered farmhouse near Stratford-upon-Avon where Shakespeare's wife grew up.

Inside, it's a rambling warren of a place, with massive hand-hewn beams, low doors, and unexpected steps. The six-teenth-century oak furniture is genuine and the costumed "Tudor wenches" (to quote the brochure) do a good job of explaining how various long-forgotten artifacts — leather bottles, trenchermen's boards, rush-candle holders, and the like — were used.

The cottage's quaint, undulating roof is surprisingly thick; the last thatching job consumed five hectares of winter wheat from the Saanich Peninsula! The leaded windows look out onto a pleasant English garden and a recreated Elizabethan village, complete with pillory.

Antique-lovers should continue through the "village" to the Olde England Inn, where more pieces are on display, and where afternoon tea is served daily.

On the grounds of the Olde England Inn, Lampson Street via Esquimalt Road. July to mid-September hours are 9 AM – 8 PM; shorter in the off-season.

Royal London Wax Museum
470 Belleville Street   *388-4461*

Housed in the former Canadian Pacific Railway steamship ticket office (yet another Rattenbury building), this attraction offers some 260 wax figures in various tableaux. While the costumes are authentic-looking and the supporting memorabilia well chosen, visitors may find some of the better-known contemporary figures a little unconvincing.

The much-touted Chamber of Horrors, which appears unchanged since I first saw it 35 years ago, proved a good deal less horrifying than a rather incongruous display nearby of surgeon's tools from a First World War field hospital.

Monarchists should be delighted, though, at the museum's replicas of England's Crown Jewels, and the extensive "Royalty Row" (even if Princess Diana, with her Marilyn Monroe-esque bosom, would have to be categorized as anatomically incorrect). There is now a chilly distance between

Diana and Prince Charles, and given the marital problems of the other younger royals, there's no telling which ex-consorts (such as Princess Anne's Mark Phillips) will have become candle fodder. From mid-May to Labour Day the hours are 9 AM – 9 PM; fall and winter they are 9:30 AM – 5 PM.

Undersea Gardens
490 Belleville Street   382-5717

Now that Sealand has drifted off, mostly due to controversies surrounding its killer whales, Undersea Gardens is now the best show in town when it comes to immersing yourself in the exotic world of our West Coast marine flora and fauna. Conveniently located at the Inner Harbour, the Gardens boasts a narrated underwater show in which a scuba diver parades some of the more interesting specimens past the viewing windows: it's a fine chance to watch octopi, wolf eels, and sturgeon in action. It also has a rehabilitation program for injured and/or abandoned harbour seals; and aside from the residents, several "free range" seals swim by regularly … particularly when it's chow time. (Undersea Gardens has also been known to offer a few unexpected laughs. One confused patron once asked, "When does this thing take off for Seattle?")

In the Inner Harbour, opposite the Parliament Buildings. Open daily, with May to Labour Day hours of 9 AM – 9 PM. In the off-season, it's open 10 AM – 5 PM.

Butterfly Gardens
1461 Benvenuto Drive (Brentwood Bay)   652-3822

Hundreds of exotic free-flying butterflies are the draw at this dreamily charming oasis of colour and calm. Sited in a large tropical greenhouse, the multi-hued stars flutter amidst lush vegetation ... and will likely oblige any camera close-ups that you have in mind. This is a fine opportunity for children to learn about the butterfly life cycle, which starts with an unattractive larva that eventually metamorphoses into one of nature's most gentle and beguiling creatures. Wheelchair accessible. Open from March till October, 9:30 AM – 5:30 PM.

Miniature World
649 Humboldt Street   385-9731

Model railroad buffs, dollhouse fanciers, and toy soldier en-

Experience the art
and culture of British
Columbia's First
Peoples in the Royal
BC Musuem

thusiasts will likely revel in the detail and extent of this attraction. Those without a passion for the petite, however, may find the thousands upon thousands of Lilliputian figures a bit, um, underwhelming. Hours vary from a summer high of 8:30 AM – 9 PM to a winter low of 9 AM – 5 PM.

MUSEUMS

Royal British Columbia Museum
675 Belleville Street   *387-3014*

Considered one of the 10 best general museums in the world, the Royal British Columbia Museum offers superb exhibits that relate the province's natural and human history. Working from a brilliant design, the museum's curators and technicians have created unforgettable displays that bring the outdoors inside, breathe life into prehistoric animals, and conjure up the sights, sounds, and smells of times past.

So enormous is the woolly mammoth looming at the entrance to the Living Land, Living Sea Gallery that nine musk ox hides had to be shipped from the Arctic to cover him. And it's just about impossible to imagine dioramas any more convincing than this museum's evocations of forest, seashore, and river delta. The trees, for instance, were cast in fibreglass in latex molds taken from living specimens, then painstakingly handpainted. The museum artists received their greatest compliment, perhaps, when one of them found a group of watercolourists at their easels in front of the seashore diorama!

Children's favourite part of the museum has always been the Modern History Gallery's uncannily realistic "Old Town." Here they can sniff an apple pie cooking in the turn-of-the-century kitchen, giggle at Charlie Chaplin in the movie house, or hear — and almost feel — a night-time freight train thundering past the tiny station.

In the First People's Gallery, displays of Aboriginal skills — fishing, whaling, blanket-weaving, and woodworking — lead up to a magnificent scale model, five years in the making, of the now-abandoned Haida village of Skedans, in the Queen Charlotte Islands. Most visitors find this gallery to be extremely moving and thought-provoking.

To sum it up, this outstanding museum is a true "must see," one of the very best things Victoria has to offer. A family pass is a bargain at $10.70.

One block south of the Empress Hotel. Open daily except Christmas and New Year's. July 1 to September 8 the hours are 9:30 AM – 7 PM; winter hours are 10 AM – 5:30 PM.

Maritime Museum of B.C.
28 Bastion Square   385-4222

Bordered by the sea on three sides, and home to a major naval base for some 130 years, Victoria has an important maritime history. The Maritime Museum, located in the former Provincial Court House (recently declared a national historic site), relates the story of this region's merchant and naval shipping, from the time of the early explorers to the present day.

The large ground-floor gallery houses *Trekka*, a 6-metre ketch sailed around the world solo in the 1950s, and *Tilikum*, an odd conversion of a 11-metre First Nations dugout canoe, which made a two-year passage from Victoria to England at the turn of the century.

Hard by these vessels, you'll find models and paintings of "tall ships," a whaling display, and a selection of sailors' art, including fancy rope braiding, decorated ostrich eggs, and, of course, ships in bottles. The second-floor galleries contain a history of Captain Cook's voyages (with some superb eighteenth-century globes), models and memorabilia of the elegant Canadian Pacific *Empress* and *Princess* ships, and naval artifacts, uniforms, and photos.

While the museum used to be rather an old-fashioned one — in the "glass case and label" tradition — it is in the middle of a comprehensive million-dollar renovation and revitalization that will add an extra 3,000 square metres of gallery space and transform it into the province's most exciting marine exhibition centre. The renovation will be finished by 1998.

One of the new galleries, Kids' Zone, will feature interactive exhibits that should fire any child's imagination. And sea dogs of any age should set aside an entire afternoon to take in everything properly. The gift shop offers an excellent selection of nautical books.

The Maritime Museum is open 9:30 AM – 4:30 PM daily.

Craigdarroch Castle
1050 Joan Crescent   *592-5323*

Without a doubt the grandest and most picturesque private home ever built in western Canada, Craigdarroch Castle looks like it has just dropped in from a fairy tale. This turreted marvel, with its steep, red tile roof and seven towering chimneys, was completed in 1890, the gift of coal baron Robert Dunsmuir to his wife, Joan.

In 1869, near Nanaimo, Dunsmuir had personally discovered the legendary Wellington coal seam. It made him the province's first millionaire and allowed him to lavish some $500,000 on this opulent residence, built in the Scottish Baronial style. Sadly, Dunsmuir died before he could inhabit his Xanadu.

After Joan Dunsmuir's death in 1908 the castle became first a lottery prize (!) and then served variously as a military hospital, college campus, office building, and conservatory of music. In recent years, the Craigdarroch Castle Historical Museum Society has been gradually refurnishing the castle (now owned by the city), with loving attention to detail. No settee, ottoman, or Victorian *bibelot* on display dates from later than 1890. The society has even tracked down the Dunsmuirs' original

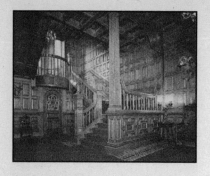

Stately Craigdarroch
Castle offers a rare
glimpse of Victoria's
early grandeur
(*Nigel Drever*)

Steinway grand, and several of their paintings.

The society's volunteer docents offer continual guided tours,
after which visitors may linger to indulge any particular interest. The castle's stained glass windows are among the finest
secular examples in North America. (A leaded Sir Walter
Raleigh surveys the smoking room approvingly.) The entrance
hall features golden oak panelling, prefabricated in Chicago,
and an exquisite inlaid floor justifies the society's plea — "no
stiletto heels." Above all, don't miss climbing the 87 steps to
the north turret, for one of the city's finest views. Hours from
mid-June to Labour Day are 9 AM – 7 PM; during winter they
are 10 AM – 4:30 PM. Access is via Fort Street, up the hill and
due east of downtown.

Fort Rodd Hill/Fisgard Lighthouse
603 Fort Rodd Hill Road   478-5849

Fort Rodd Hill's three gun batteries were constructed in the
late 1890s to protect what was then a Royal Navy base on
Esquimalt Harbour. Until coastal artillery defences were declared obsolete in 1956, the fort was part of an extensive net-
work of gun batteries, searchlights, and observation posts in
the Victoria-Esquimalt area.

You needn't be an artillery buff, though, to enjoy this beautiful 18-hectare waterfront park and its spectacular views. Families often stay for half a day, since, in addition to the
fortifications, there are beaches, tidepools, and forest trails to
explore. In the summer, park interpreters give various demon-
strations, and the canteen is open. And if you're lucky, some of
the park's Columbian blacktail deer may come out to graze.

The Fisgard
Lighthouse, one of
our oldest landmarks
(*Jeff Barber, INFocus
Photography*)

Near the fort, a causeway leads to Fisgard Lighthouse, built
in 1860 as the first permanent light on the B.C. coast. Displays
inside the former keeper's house include maps, models, a variety of lamps and lenses, and period photos of lighthouses and
shipwrecks.

West on Craigflower Road (Highway 1A). Follow signs.
Open daily from March 1 to October 31, 10 AM – 5:30 PM, and
in the winter on weekends and during the Christmas school
vacation, 9 AM – 4:30 PM. Admission is $3 for adults, $7.50
per family. You may find it useful to combine Fort Rodd Hill
with a visit to Royal Roads University (see **Gardens and
Parks**), which is only a five-minute drive away.

Craigflower Farmhouse
110 Island Highway   *383-4627, 361-0021*

The Hudson's Bay Company's lease of lands on Vancouver
Island required it to colonize the area. Craigflower Farmhouse
was built in the mid-1850s for Kenneth McKenzie, the bailiff
of a 360-hectare farm established by the Puget Sound Agricultural Company, a subsidiary of the HBC.

Costumed interpreters now conduct tours of the convincingly refurnished rooms. Highlights include the kitchen, with
its collection of curious implements, and the fireplaces — angled into the corner in the living and dining rooms, and Gothic
arched in some of the bedrooms.

The house enjoys a pleasant view of the Gorge waterway
and the nearby Colonial Schoolhouse, the oldest in western
Canada.

Open daily 11 AM – 5 PM from mid-May to mid-October,

and noon – 4 PM in the off-season. Admission is $4 for adults, $10 per family. Head up Government, turning left at Craigflower, which eventually becomes Highway 1A. Craigflower Farmhouse is at the corner of Craigflower and Admirals.

Point Ellice House
2616 Pleasant Street   *380-6506*

Located in what was once one of the city's finest waterfront residential districts, Point Ellice House now nestles like a genteel gem amidst rock-crushing yards and mountains of junk cars. But don't let the neighbourhood put you off. The heritage redwoods and arbutuses around the property block out all but a scenic view of the Gorge waterway.

The house itself, a rambling, pastel-coloured 1861 bungalow, was home to three generations of the O'Reilly family, and still contains a fine collection of their Victoriana. Over the years, house guests such as Sir John A. Macdonald (Canada's first prime minister) and Scott of the Antarctic sipped tea — more likely whiskey — in front of the marble fireplace.

After being guided through the house by costumed interpreters, you can retire to the garden to admire the nineteenth-century rosebushes, or perhaps get in a spot of croquet on the lawn. Tea, served noon – 4 PM, is $9.95 for "high tea" and $5.95 for a lighter repast; phone for reservations at 380-6506.

Open daily 10 AM – 5 PM from mid-May to Labour Day. Closed in the off-season. Admission is $4 for adults.

Helmcken House
#10 Elliot Street Square   *387-4697*

This cosy house, the oldest in B.C. still open to the public, was built on its present site in 1852 for Dr. J.S. Helmcken, one of Victoria's first medical doctors and a son-in-law of Governor James Douglas. Helmcken lived here until his death in 1920, at age 95. His surgical tools and medicine bottles, which are on display, constitute one of Canada's finest nineteenth-century medical collections. The period furnishings — many original to the house — and the informative costumed interpreters make this a pleasant minor attraction.

Open daily 11 AM – 5 PM from mid-May to mid-September; hours reduced to noon 4 – PM in the off-season. Admission is

$4 for adults, $10 per family. Helmcken House is located immediately behind the Royal B.C. Museum, between Belleville and Superior.

Carr House
207 Government Street 383-5843

This attractive 1863 Italianate-style house was the birthplace of Victoria's most famous artist, Emily Carr. Although restoration is still in progress, the exquisitely refurnished and repapered rooms will offer much to lovers of Victoriana. The tour by a costumed guide includes interesting details about the search through Emily's writings for clues as to the house's original interior.

Hours are 10 AM – 5 PM from mid-May to mid-October; group tours are available year-round. Admission is $4 for adults, $10 for the family.

HISTORIC BUILDINGS

Parliament Buildings
501 Belleville Street 387-3046

Plans by the 25-year-old architect Francis Rattenbury won the competition to design these magnificent buildings, home to B.C.'s Legislative Assembly. Built over five years, at a cost of close to a million dollars, they opened in 1898.

Some of the more than 3,000 lightbulbs that outline the buildings at night have never been replaced (except at Christmastime, when those on the dome are changed to red and green).

Though some may find the rather formal guided tour of the rotunda area a bit too much like a civics class, it does take you past some fine mosaics, marble, woodwork, and stained glass. And if at any point you hear what sounds like an unruly seventh-grade class whose teacher has left the room, it merely means that our legislature is in session.

The half-hour tours run year-round, and hit a peak during July and August, when they go every 20 minutes. Tours can be conducted in English, French, German, Cantonese, Mandarin, Spanish, and some other languages (depending on who's been hired that summer). Please phone to confirm on the morning you wish to tour, particularly if you need a foreign-language guide. Admission free.

Royal Roads University
2005 Sooke Road   *391-2511*

Please see write-up in **Gardens and Parks**.

Thunderbird Park
Corner of Belleville and Douglas

Over the years, Thunderbird Park has been filled with totem poles carved and painted by Native artists employed by the nearby Royal British Columbia Museum. In the summer you can watch these master carvers at work, and inhale the glorious smell of fresh cedar as their chisels and adzes make the chips fly. Open daily. Admission free.

Christ Church Cathedral
Quadra at Rockland   *383-2714*

Not all the great churches are in Europe! Christ Church Cathedral, built in the late 1920s in thirteenth-century Gothic style, is one of the country's largest churches and certainly the most impressive in Victoria. The cathedral's campanologists occasionally gather at the base of the north tower — which, like its southern twin, rises 37 metres — to ring the changes on the fine set of bells, a replica of those at Westminster Abbey. Not even the bells, however, can awaken the residents of Pioneer Square, across the road to the north. This was Victoria's first cemetery, begun in the days of the Hudson's Bay Company fort. Beneath its venerable oaks you'll find the simple sandstone markers of fur traders and Royal Navy sailors.

Hours are 8:30 AM – 5:30 PM, Monday to Saturday, and 7:30 AM – 8:30 PM on Sunday. Admission free.

Dominion Astrophysical Observatory
5071 West Saanich Road   *383-0001*

Canada's National Research Council operates this facility, equipped with a large-diameter telescope that allows astronomers to explore the farthest reaches of the universe. Stargazers of any age will enjoy the striking photos of galaxies and nebulae displayed in the base of the dome. Those preferring a more terrestrial aspect can step outside for great views of Victoria and its surrounding hills.

Open daily, 9:15 AM – 4:30 PM. Open for public stargazing in the summer, 9 PM – 11 PM Saturdays. Admission free. Drive

north from Victoria on Highway 17, take the exit for Royal
Oak, then head north again on West Saanich Road.

SIGHTSEEING TOURS

Black Beauty Line Victorian Carriage Tours
361-1220

Take the James Bay/Beacon Hill/Dallas Road tour in these traditional horse-drawn carriages, which hold up to six adults.
There are four different routes, ranging from 15 minutes up to
one hour. Their season typically runs from mid-March through
to the end of October, and operating hours are 9:30 AM till 11
PM (those atmospheric night rides through the park are great).
Reservations are taken, but nearly all their business is walk-by;
tours start from the corner of Menzies and Belleville, just up
from the Legislative Buildings at the Inner Harbour.

Capital City Tally-Ho
383-5067

In turn-of-the-century Victoria, a horse-drawn Tally-Ho was
just an ordinary form of public transport. From about 1940,
though, these Belgian-drawn carriages have been clip-clopping
through the streets solely for the benefit of tourists. They move
slowly, which means that you get to savour all the sights (including the occasional grimaces of grumpy locals who *just want
to get home*). The Tally-Ho takes up to 20 passengers, and does
an hour route through James Bay, Beacon Hill Park, and the
Dallas Road waterfront. The season runs April through October, and the daily hours are 10 AM till 7 PM. Tickets on sale at
the corner of Belleville and Menzies, just up from the Legislative Buildings

Cooper Air Inc.
Victoria Airport (Sidney)   *656-3968*

If you don't just want to "follow the birds to Victoria," but
desire to sprout wings of your own, charter a float plane and
get some wonderful sky-high views of southwestern British
Columbia. Cooper Air offers a wide range of tour options, some
of which are naturalist led. A simple aerial tour of Victoria takes
a half-hour ($65); their most elaborate adventure lasts nearly
four hours and costs $395 per person.

Gray Line
388-5248

These are the double-decker beauties that are always chugging
through the streets of Victoria. Their "Grand City Tour" is a
90-minute cruise, which hits Oak Bay, Craigdarroch Castle,
and the Lieutenant-Governor's House. The ever-popular
Butchart Gardens tour, running May-September, is scheduled
for three hours (but you can stay longer in the Gardens and
catch a later bus back … assuming there's a seat for you). During the summer, the Grand City buses leave about every
half-hour, from 9 AM till 5:30 PM; and from October through
April, they leave at noon and 2 PM. The Butchart Gardens'
buses leave hourly, from 9 AM till 7 PM. Ticket sales and bus
departures are directly in front of the Empress Hotel.

Heritage Tours
713 Bexhill Road   *474-4332*

For $60 an hour you can take a luxury tour of the city, lan-
guidly reclining in a six-seater Daimler limo (the "ultra-stretch"
that seats 10 goes for $70). These flexible guided tours range
from the "Grand City Tour" (heritage mansions, Beach Drive,
and Craigdarroch Castle for 75 minutes) to that same tour plus
an in-depth guided prowl through Craigdarroch, totalling two
hours. They also can do a customized "Heritage Homes" jaunt,
and often waft high-rollers away to outlying luxury restaurants
such as the Deep Cove Chalet. They also offer a two-and-a-
half-hour visit to Butchart Gardens (including 90 minutes
amidst the blooms).

Kabuki Cabs
385-4243

For a less formal downtown tour — or just as an excuse to
spare those sore feet a painful trudge back to the hotel — listen
for the cheery, jingly bells of a white Kabuki Cab soliciting a
customer. Basically, these pedicabs are bike-powered rickshaws,
and they scoot through Victoria streets, powered by tanned and
muscular legs that are a lot stronger than yours. The riders are
trained to give historical tours, so learn some architectural and
social history at your leisure. The rates are a dollar a minute.
Kabuki season is April through September, and they operate
between 9 AM and 3 AM.

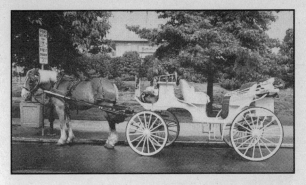

Victoria Carriage Tours clip-clop leisurely through the scenic areas of old Victoria

Whale Watching
See **Ecotourism**.

Victoria Carriage Tours
383-2207

These classic, all-white, horse-drawn carriages wend their romantic way through Beacon Hill Park, James Bay, and the waterfront (the four different tours range from 30 to 90 minutes). They carry a maximum of six passengers, and operate year-round; summer hours are 8 AM – 11 PM, while winter hours are 10 AM – 10 PM. Tickets and departure point are located at the corner of Menzies and Belleville, just up from the Legislative Buildings.

Harbour Tours
480-0971

Since Victoria is bounded on water by three sides, it only makes sense to consider getting off the pavement for a salmon-eye view of the city. Those interested in a touch of the exotic can cruise in the black gondola that leaves irregularly from the Inner Harbour (there's even a tame seal that often tags along in hopes of cadging a mackerel or two off the captain). Tickets can be purchased on-site or from the Tourist Bureau at the north end of the Harbour.

The other option is to catch a ride on one of the dozen tugboat-shaped Victoria Harbour Ferries that travel a circuit of 10

Our harbour ferries offer intriguing marine tours of Victoria

stops throughout Victoria's harbour (stops range from Fisherman's Wharf and West Bay Marina to Ocean Pointe Resort and
Chinatown). For adults a single "hop" costs $2.50, but don't
overlook the 45-minute tour of the Inner and Outer Harbours,
which costs $10. They also do a moonlight cruise for $8, and a
50-minute tour of Victoria's historic and stately Gorge Waterway for $12.

ECOTOURISM

Ecotourism is one of the most exciting options for visitors to Victoria. A good starting point is the **Victoria Marine Adventure Centre** (950 Wharf Street, 995-2211), which is a broker for about 20 companies selling everything from whale-watching tours and scuba diving to rock climbing and seaplane excursions. Some companies offer flexible packages, including full-day combinations of kayaking and hiking: truly a memorable way to experience the wild beauty of southern B.C.

WHALE WATCHING

A whale-watching excursion could well be the single most exciting thing you do in Victoria: "It was the experience of a lifetime" is a common comment heard by the staff of the tour companies. Three pods comprising approximately 100 killer whales make their home in the coastal waters off Victoria — thus making it the world's largest population of resident whales. Although whale sightings aren't absolutely guaranteed — unless you carry a pager and can become available on short notice once a pod has been spotted — the best companies boast an 85 percent success rate in summer. And even if those magnificent mammals don't appear, your 50- to 80-kilometre tour will give you lots of stunning photo opportunities with seals, porpoises, sea lions, tugboats, log booms — in all, an unforgettable portrait of the West Coast.

Victoria now has about a dozen whale-watching operations; however, many of the newer operators lack experience and sophisticated tracking gear. Three of the established companies are **Seacoast Expeditions** (383-2254); **Five Star Charters** (388-7223); and **Ocean Explorations** (383-ORCA).

Whale watching could be the highlight of your trip *(Ken Baccomb)*

KAYAKING/SAILING

Kayakers interested in an unforgettable expedition can spend anything from two days to more than a week exploring the 100 islands and islets that compose the **Broken Islands Group,** a unique wilderness area at the entrance to Barkley Sound. The Broken Islands are best accessed via Ucluelet, a West Coast fishing village about a five-hour drive from Victoria. This is a superb opportunity for kayakers to float off into a different reality. Those who prefer sailpower might want to book with **Seahorse Sailing** (2075A Tryon, 655-4979), a boat-chartering company offering a two-week circumnavigation of Vancouver Island. **Blackfish Wilderness Expeditions** (721-1882) also offers a choice of tours in a 14-metre cedar whaling canoe; seal and cormorant colonies, uninhabited islands, and undisturbed reefs are all on the itinerary.

BIKES & HIKES

Three-day guided bike tours of Victoria and southern Vancouver Island are available through **Greenday Bicycle Tours** (380-6033). Serious hikers have two choices: either the venerable West Coast Trail (see below) or the brand-new Juan de Fuca Marine Trail, 47 kilometres of coast-hugging, sweat-inducing splendour that spans Jordan River north to Port Renfrew (a brochure is available from B.C. Parks at 391-2300). Although

Juan de Fuca is a three- to four-day jaunt, it's easy to do part of
the trail as a day trip. Best access is at either terminus: China
Beach, 2 kilometres west of Jordan River and a 90-minute
drive from Victoria; or Botanical Beach, a provincial park just
west of Port Renfrew.

Although Botanical Beach is an extra 40 kilometres, it's
well worth the effort: at low tide there is an extraordinary and
diverse profusion of intertidal lifeforms such as starfish, acorn
barnacles, limpets, sea urchins, and anemones on display in
tidepools carved out of a long sandstone shelf. (Head up the
Old Island Highway past Sooke; when you reach Port Renfrew go to the end of West Coast Road. And to make sure that
your visit coincides with low tide, check out a tide table by
phoning an outdoors store or looking in the "weather alma-
nac" section of the daily *Times-Colonist*.)

PACIFIC RIM NATIONAL PARK

Welcome to Canada's first-ever "national marine park." This
world-class ecological preserve has three distinct parts: Long
Beach, the 13-kilometre stretch of sand and surf that offers
dazzling views of the open Pacific (even when it's raining,
which is often!); the Broken Islands Group, which affords a
unique environment for kayakers and wilderness campers; and
the West Coast Trail, a 72-kilometre hike that evolved out of a
turn-of-the- century "life saving trail" that was installed because of the numerous ships that cracked up on the area's treach-
erous shores. (It's a five-hour drive to Long Beach. Head up
the Trans- Canada, turning left onto Highway 4 just south of
Parksville; head west towards Ucluelet.)

Long Beach
Set between the small fishing villages of Ucluelet to the south
and Tofino to the north, sublimely primordial Long Beach is a
paradise to surfers and beachcombers alike. The beach and
various headlands and woodland trails will keep hikers happy
for many hours, while water babies who don't mind a chill can
take their measure of this big ocean. And whale watching is a
seasonal activity that is increasingly popular up here, due to
the huge migrating greys who snack off-shore (prime time is
mid-March to mid-April).

Campers will be lucky to get into the Green Point Campsite, which operates on a first come, first served basis. There are also campgrounds near Tofino. People who prefer to camp in the great indoors can choose from hotels in the town of Ucluelet, several resorts spotted along Highway 4 south of Tofino, and in Tofino itself.

This area has a rich Native heritage. One must-see is the Eagle Aerie Gallery, a longhouse-style building featuring the works of internationally celebrated artist Roy Vickers. (And while you're in Tofino, look up the West Coast Maritime Museum, corner of Third Street and Campbell Avenue.)

WEST COAST TRAIL

Although not for the casual hiker, this challenging route has been taken by both children and old age pensioners. Slow travellers can spend up to a week travelling between Bamfield in the north and Port Renfrew in the south. If you want to be one of the more than 5,000 happy campers who tackle this rewarding scramble, do ensure that you're equipped for rainy weather and some pretty steep slopes. (And make some kind of arrangements to have a second vehicle or a pick-up party waiting when you and your blistered feet emerge back in civilization.) And hikers who just want a day's taste of this trail can begin at Pachena and hike to Nitinat Narrows, then retrace their steps.

Due to excessive use, a reservation system now controls access to the Trail. Reservations are a pre-requisite for hiking, and can be obtained by phoning 1-800-663-6000. (Note: reservations are not necessary for day hikers.)

SHOPPING

People who love to shop should have quite a fling while they're in Victoria. Whether you want just a souvenir T-shirt or are prepared to invest in $20,000 worth of Georgian silverware, Victoria's retail businesses will be delighted to have you as a customer. Because the downtown core is set to pedestrian scale, this shopping guide organizes its shops by geographic area and not by category. There are five separate sections: Government Street, Old Town, Downtown, Antique Row, and Chinatown. The least ambitious of Victoria's shops get no mention in this guide; those with some personality or special products or services are referred to in passing. Shops of particular merit receive a more extensive write-up.

GOVERNMENT STREET

The brick-pavement Government Street promenade, from the Inner Harbour five blocks up to the beginning of Old Town, is the heartland of Victorian shopping. From British woollens and fine bone china to Cowichan Indian sweaters and chocolate creams nearly the size of hockey pucks, there's a cornucopia of consumer goods to choose from. There is also a proliferation of lower-end souvenir parlours, most of which sell the same cotton sweaters, gaudy miniature totem poles, and presentation bottles of maple syrup — hey, they don't call it "tourist row" for nothing! Many of Victoria's best shops can be found elsewhere in the city, so don't blow out your Mastercard limit before having a good look-round.

If you can get past the clutter of "cute" pottery knick-knacks at **Sydney Reynolds** (801 Government Street, 383-3931), this vintage Victoria store has some prize porcelain and crystal to offer. Across the street there's an equal mix of kitsch and quality at the **Custom House Art Gallery** (801 Wharf Street, 381-1022), including some interesting West Coast ceramics and a good selection of aboriginal art (framed silkscreens can cost $1,000; that man-sized totem pole goes for $2,000 a foot). **Timber Ridge** (817 Government Street, 384-1897) has some interesting outdoor clothing and some rainsticks hidden in the back. **Prescott & Andrews** (909 Government Street, 384-2515), a trove of British knitwear, is just the place for sweater fanatics.

Rogers' Chocolates
913 Government Street   *384-7021*

Some visitors head first for the Parliament Buildings, others for high tea at the Empress; but the connoisseurs of candy make an undignified rush to pay homage at Rogers' Chocolates, one of the world's most respected shrines to the sweet tooth. Charles "Candy" Rogers started selling his goodies more than a century ago; today his legendary Victoria Creams get shipped around the world ... including to Buckingham Palace and the White House. Along with the 15 flavours of creams, Rogers' also sells chews, candy, and an award-winning almond cluster out of its quaintly Victorian shop. A must-visit.

Scottish sweaters are the biggest seller at the **Edinburgh Tartan Shop** (921 Government Street, 388-9312), but they also stock motoring blankets, kilts and kilt pins (with authentic clan crests), and more than 50 tartan fabrics by the yard. Across the way at **Artina's Jewellery** (1002 Government Street, 386-7000), there's an emphasis on the best of West Coast artists. Styles range from exotic porcelain and chunky pieces of carved mastodon ivory inlaid with black coral, lapis, and turquoise, to extravagant and playful floral necklaces made from fimo, an acrylic clay, and gorgeous Indian silverwork. **Avoca Handweavers** (1009 Government Street, 383-043), is a fine shop specializing in Irish imports: beautiful sweaters, Celtic-design jewellery, Guinness memorabilia, funky cloth caps, mohair throw rugs, and woollen capes, jackets, and skirts. There's even a small collection of Irish literature and music for sale.

Hill's Indian Crafts
1008 Government Street 385-3911

Don't overlook this great shop, one of Victoria's two best out-
lets for quality aboriginal art. Hill's has been in business for 50
years and represents many of the greatest artists from most of
B.C.'s coastal nations. The shop has everything from dream
catchers, drums, and talking sticks to carved paddles, wooden
carvings, and a great selection of Haida argillite and silver jewellery. They also have some unusual items for sale, including
button blankets and bentwood boxes. If you want that Coast
Salish "welcoming pole" carved from red cedar, better have a
spare $11,000 in your wallet.

————————

Fans of aboriginal art shouldn't overlook **Eagle's Moon
Gallery** (1010 Government Street, 361-4184), which showcases the work of Roy Henry Vickers, one of B.C.'s most celebrated and successful artists. The cedar walls and dim lighting
effectively create the mood of a longhouse. A few doors up is
Northern Passage (1020 Government Street, 381-3380), an
attractive store featuring Inuit sculpture, Indian silver jewellery, contemporary ceramics, and paintings. Those with a taste
for old-country craftsmanship can investigate **Irish Linen
Stores** (1019 Government Street, 383-6812), which has been
selling fine cotton, linen, and lace products since 1910. Although they favour Irish goods, these direct importers also sell
quality linens from Belgium and Switzerland.

Victoria, amazingly, has three Christmas stores — maybe
we should drop the "little bit of Olde England" shtick and go
with a Santa/North Pole theme instead. Those in yule with-
drawal can visit the **Spirit of Christmas** (1022 Government,
385-2501) and stuff their stockings with everything from $300
woven vine wreaths to all-cotton night shirts featuring skating
pigs and less irreverent Christmas iconography.

————————

Munro's Books
1108 Government Street 382-2464

Sited in a beautifully restored 1909 heritage building, Munro's
is possibly the most stunning bookstore in the country. The

Munro's Books:
one of the most
beautiful bookstores
in Canada
(*Jeff Barber, INFocus
Photography*)

cathedral-like atmosphere, with its coffered ceiling, stained glass windows, and contemporary fabric murals, is wonderfully conducive to a leisurely browse … and with 35,000 titles in stock, you may be here awhile! Knowledgeable and pleasant staff.

———————

Worth a visit just for the intoxicating smell of fresh-roast that pervades this tasteful coffee emporium, **Murchie's** (1110 Government Street, 383-3112) also has a grand selection of fine china, silver, and crystal. And want a cigar to go with that pound of Kenyan AA? Even if you abhor the tobacco vice, drop in on **E.A. Morris** (1116 Government Street, 382-4811), a century-old smoker's paradise. E.A. Morris ships its pipe blends around the world; it also sells Cuban cigars and a panoply of pipes that include elaborately carved meerschaums.

———————

British Importers
138 Eaton Centre   *386-1496*

This dress-for-success men's clothing store has been selling power suits and upmarket casual gear to tourists and locals alike for decades. The store won a national design award, but take your eyes off the handmade lighting fixtures long enough to admire what's hanging jauntily on the racks. Those drop-dead threads by Boss, Klein, and Zegna cost up to $1,300 per suit; the dress shirts and sportier lines are priced accordingly. British Importers favours European fabrics, with an emphasis on softer silhouettes and a comfortable cut. The notable leather jackets and delirious ties are also worth a look. BI puts out its own quarterly mini-magazine (it's surprisingly readable) and offers good value.

———————

Keep going past block-long **Eaton Centre**, a monument to North American consumerism with four floors of typical mall fare including the **Eaton's** department store, then turn right up View Street for three fine shops. **Pomegranate** (614 View Street, 388-0488) is like visiting an upmarket African-Asian bazaar: there's funkily exotic clothing (tribal patterns, batiks, etc.) as well as a wide selection of objêts d'art to spice up a living room dominated by too much Scandinavian furniture. Don't be fooled by all the bronze carp balanced on their tails and a selection of framed Oriental paintings that make the place resemble an Asian gallery: **MacDonald Jewellery** (618 View Street, 382-4113) is a grand place to hunt for rings and pearls. Ian MacDonald designs and makes all his own jewellery, specializing in precious gems such as sapphires, rubies, and emeralds ("You can still get a nice coloured stone in the $500 range"), and unusual diamond cuts like squares and triangles. Styles include the traditional on out to wacky high-fashion fun jewellery. And fans of the hopeful spirit of New Age should visit **Instinct Art & Gifts** (622 View Street, 388-5033), where the more predictable crystals and other such "healing" gear keep company with gargoyles, wind chimes, drums, and other such well-chosen esoterica.

Contemporary fashion is the buzz in **Breeze** (1150 Government Street, 383-8871), where the high-tech environment and a high-energy staff pass on the colourful spirit of Esprit, which they sell exclusively. More conservative fashion finds a home at **Polo** (1200 Government Street, 381-7656), where Ralph

Lauren's classic plaids, earthy colours, and fine craftsmanship seem to evoke the spirit of a mythical American gentry.

At this point there's another brief detour: left to Bastion Square or right to Trounce Alley. **Bastion Square**, original site of Fort Victoria (look for the freestanding archway), consists mostly of offices and some restaurants; it's also notable for its outdoor market, which proliferates with such bohemian-flavoured items as candles, funky clothing, jewellery, and aboriginal art. Look also for **Dig This** (45 Bastion Square, 385-3212), which is a must-visit for all dedicated gardeners. And just up from the Square is **Designs for Dining** (1218 Langley Street, 383-3569), a browsing experience for people who like to live in beauty (with a touch of whimsy on the side). Items include pottery (functional to outrageous), handmade furniture (pine tables and chests, maple chairs done in a traditional Quebec country style), high-tech wine racks and CD holders executed in metal, jute rugs, raku, elaborate candlestick holders, steel coffee tables, and lots of original art work.

Venerable **Trounce Alley** offers some great shopping. **Nushin Boutique** (606 Trounce Alley, 381-2131) is one of Victoria's most elite women's clothing stores and it stocks the leading edge in European design. Confident — and rich — shoppers will do well here. **All In Bloom** (616 Trounce Alley, 383-1883) offers the final word on gifts with a floral theme. Aside from a large selection of vases and other obvious items they also have hand-cast paper cards (bas-reliefs made from antique moulds), *kenzan* vases for Japanese flower arrangments, French-wired ribbons, citronella garden torches shaped like vegetables and gladiolas, Shaker-style picnic baskets, and cotton blankets patterned either like tapestries or the illustrations from Victorian children's books. Definitely worth a visit. And if you subscribe to *Gourmet*, then check out **Haute Cuisine** (1210 Broad Street, 388-9906) for its fine selection of fancy cookware, arty ceramics, and library of cookbooks.

In business since the 1860s, **W. & J. Wilson** (1221 Government Street, 383-7177) still believes in selling quality clothing that is sensible instead of sensational. Their men's section stocks the classic British designers such as Hardy Amies, Burberry, and Daks; the women's half of the store favours European designers. The threads get notably more trendy next door in **Anthony James** (1225 Government Street, 381-2152), which features the latest looks from Europe, especially Italy. This store showcases innovative design and quality fabrics. And for people who want to *look* like they're headed for the great outdoors, prep your expedition in **Eddie Bauer** (1254 Government Street, 383-1964). Shoppers looking for a good selection of Cowichan Indian sweaters or fiercely beautiful tribal masks can take their wampum to **Sasquatch Trading** (1233 Government Street, 386-9033), one of Victoria's better Indian crafts emporiums. Those more interested in high-end denim (Diesel and Pepe spoken here) and trendy casual wear can take a walk in **Street** (1241 Government Street, 383-0424).

OLD TOWN

Victoria's so-called Old Town area is our most successful effort at preserving the past while maintaining a sense of ongoing life and zest. These several blocks just north of the original Fort Victoria have been handsomely restored, yet are brimming with contemporary vitality in the form of ethnic restaurants, a brewpub, unique boutiques, and a giant "market" containing over 40 shops and businesses. Local developer Michael Williams won an international heritage development award for his extensive work along lower Yates and Johnson; those renewed facades, with their rich detailing and strong colours, lend Victoria some of its most confident and authentic charm.

Dovetail Furniture & Folk Art
1252 Wharf Street   *920-0168*

Browsers will love the colourful, ultra-whimsical folk art pieces here: there are sly whirligigs, life-size mounties, crocodiles with beer caps for scales, foot stools disguised as cats and pelicans. They also have rustic antique furniture, "naive" paintings, and lots of other stuff you don't *need* (but will probably want to own).

Carnaby Street
538 Yates Street   *382-3747*

Funk and colour are the raison d'etre of this unique store, which has been selling extravagant folk art, antique and new tribal jewellery, handmade ethnic clothes, and Oriental carpets since the tie-dyed glory days of 1968. Owners Rosina Izzard and Robert Usatch spent years travelling South America and the globe; they developed not only trading contacts, but actual work co-ops to produce garments unique to the store. Rosina studied archaeology at the University of Mexico before becoming an entrepreneur; the first cottage industry she initiated employed destitute and handicapped women in India. Currently, Carnaby Street supports several hundred families in Central and South America, who keep the store stocked with hand-spun and dyed sweaters, colourful scarves and socks, and other antidotes to high-fashion glitz.

"Bohemian arts & rags" reads the sign for **Hughes** (564 Yates Street, 381-4405), and this offbeat and upscale clothing boutique makes good on that promise to deliver designer fashion for men and women. It features contemporary chic from Canadian and European designers, with an emphasis on casual wear. There's a whiff of pretension about **Mirari** (576 Yates Street, 380-1114), but it's definitely worth a peek: all those high-design objêts d'art, arty glassware, and faux-rustic wooden furniture seem preeningly ready for a photo spread in *Home Beautiful*.

Atman Bookstore (1308 Government Street, 383-3032) specializes in metaphysical and New Age books, videotapes featuring some of today's popular gurus, crystals and "healing stones," cards, calendars, and tarot decks: the waft of incense, coupled with the soothing sounds of meditation music, make Sri Atman a singularly pleasant spot to browse. At **Chinook Trading** (1315 Government Street, 383-7021) a fine selection of B.C. First Nations arts and crafts is available to the discerning collector and the souvenir-seeker alike. Prices range from $10 for a beaded necklace to $25,000 for a totem pole. And if there's room in your sleigh, go shopping in **The Original Christmas Village** (1323 Government Street, 380-7552), which features a beguiling collection of glittering baubles, figurines, and bric-a-brac that is mostly traditional German.

Well-made casual clothing is the raison d'etre of **The Gap** (1319 Government Street, 920-9925), and its Victoria store is well stocked and nicely laid out. Clothing is a bit more robust at the adjoining **Pacific Trekking** (1305 Government Street,

388-7088). Things take a turn to the whimsical at **Kaboodles** (1320 Government Street, 383-0931), which has a great selection of toys, trinkets, cards, and eccentric accessories for kids of all ages. Long a downtown fixture, **Cowichan Trading Company** (1328 Government Street, 383-0321) specializes in West Coast First Nations arts and crafts: it mixes touristy T-shirts with an excellent selection of genuine Cowichan sweaters, moccasins, fine ornamental masks, animal carvings, and silver jewellery such as earrings, bracelets, necklaces, and pins.

Canadian Heritage Designs (581 Johnson Street, 388-0661) sells elegant pine furniture, throw rugs, whimsical light switch casings, glassware, old-fashioned fire irons, ceramics, and antiqued birdhouses (for $100!) — country living, in other words, for people who don't get much cow shit on their shoes. And if your lifestyle needs some colourful accessorizing, then check out **Ethos** (574 Johnson Street, 382-2131), which boasts a bounty of exotic earrings, bracelets, batik robes, huge fans, scarves, and wonderful hand-carved wooden masks, most of which come from Bali and other parts of Indonesia, as well as Thailand and Mexico.

Owned by two jazz-loving brothers-in-law, **Sweet Thunder Records** (575 Johnson Street, 381-4042) is well worth a visit if you feel that Billie Holliday and Duke Ellington were onto a good thing. There are loads of hard-to-get discs here, including specialty Japanese imports and audiophile pressings, and the knowledgeable owners will happily suggest which of the 20 early Miles Davis records are indispensable. There's free coffee for those who know who wrote "Goodbye Porkpie Hat." And don't miss **Zydeco** (565 Johnson Street, 389-1877), a whoopee cushion of a store whose mind-boggling selection of stuff, piled and stacked in gaudy disarray, includes wild and crazy T-shirts and a bumper crop of cards, mugs, glasses, toys, games, colourful note paper, and splendidly tacky costume jewellery guaranteed to tickle and tease any connoisseur of novelty items. This is an adult toy store that kids love, too.

The **Paper Box Arcade** (551 Johnson Street) is definitely worth a walk-through: it's a pretty refurbished heritage area, and there's a gorgeous slate-terraced garden that's invisible from the street. The shops not to miss include **Sacred Herb — The Hemp Shop** (106-561 Johnson Street, 384-0659), which defi-

antly celebrates marijuana and commercial products stemming
from hemp; **Still Life** (551 Johnson Street, 386-5655), which
offers vintage clothing of genuine merit — classic designs from
the '30s and '40s, some glamour gowns, and fringier fashion
statements such as bowling shirts and Hawaiian shirts in glow-
ing rayon; and **Ming Wo** (547 Johnson Street, 480-0028), which
is one of Victoria's best-equipped kitchen shops.

MARKET SQUARE

Thanks to the aggressive and visionary efforts of developer
Sam Bawlf, Victoria began to move away from its timid con-
servatism and admit that the city could be more than just an
"Olde England" theme park. His efforts resulted in Market
Square, a square block of restored heritage buildings whose
more than 40 shops constitute a shopper's mecca; they also
contribute a bustling, contemporary vitality to the city. The
strikingly landscaped inner courtyard is a great place to relax
on a bench, yoghurt cone in hand; during the summer, there
are often free classical and jazz concerts.

Just inside the entrance to Market Square is **Griffin Books**
(168-560 Johnson Street, 383-0633), a fine general interest shop
that specializes in science fiction and art books: this is the place
to fall in love with a book you never even knew existed. Further around the middle tier is **Foxglove Toys** (162-560 Johnson
Street, 383-8852), a fun store whose selection of puzzles, invisible ink kits, toy tool sets, miniature musical instruments,
plush toys, and colourful hand puppets offers the gift of imagination. For the more mature browser, diverse and beautiful **La
Cache** (108-560 Johnson Street, 384-6343), offers a profusion
of potpourris, handsomely patterned place mats, antique-style
jewellery, country comestibles like jams and preserves, brass
pots, china, glassware, soaps, candles, and funky clothes. Right
next door, **Out of Hand** (566 Johnson Street, 384-5221), consistently offers the best selection of the indigenous arts and
crafts that give B.C. its special West Coast character: there's a
wide variety of pottery and raku (both functional and high-design
art pieces), fibre wall hangings, carvings and boxes made of
wood, and some inexpensive treats such as toiletries, jams, and
heavily textured giftwrapping paper made on the Gulf Islands.

To restore some of that shopping stamina, stop in at **Fat**

Phege's Fudge Factory (134-560 Johnson Street, 383-3435), where for 25 years the store policy has been to allow anyone to leave their diet outside and make a fat-fingered grab for some of the best fudge you'll ever eat (creamy chocolate walnut is the best seller, but we're partial to the maple syrup). When strength has been regained stop in at **Ocean River Sports** (1437 Store Street, 381-4233), a hip outdoor store that specializes in kayaks but also carries a good selection of cross-country ski gear, attractive and functional leisure clothing (almost all cotton), and lots of expedition luxuries such as neck-to-toe polypropolene underwear and sun-heated portable showers. Additional shopping in Market Squre includes **Wimsey Books** (110-560 Johnson Street, 380-1764), where there is a grand selection of both new and used novels catering to the mystery and crime crowd. There's a treasure trove of good-quality silver to be unearthed at **The Silversmith** (124-560 Johnson Street, 383-7979); the **Rubber Rainbow** (9-560 Johnson Street, 388-3532) should arouse your interest with its astonishing selection of condoms; and **Hoi Polloi** (533 Pandora Avenue, 480-7822) is a perfect browse for people whose taste runs to droll cards, incredible whimsy, and amusing oddments collected from the far edge of pop culture.

CHINATOWN

Canada's oldest Chinatown got its start during the gold rush fever of the late 1850s. A second wave of Chinese immigrants came to work on the railways two decades later; by 1884 the railway was complete and there were 17,000 Chinese in Victoria — half the city's population. Although present-day Chinatown has shrivelled to one-and-a-half blocks, it is one of Victoria's most important and intriguing historic sites. The days of legal opium dens, nefarious slavetrading, gambling, and prostitution have faded (rumoured "secret tunnels" linking the Empress Hotel and the posh Union Club with Chinatown brothels were later found to be two-foot drainage pipes with which all the early downtown was laid). Faded also is the virulent racism that the Chinese met with for a half-century. The secretive, inward-looking ambience of Chinatown that so intimidated whites in the early part of this century was simply the defensive reaction of a culture under siege.

This fierce stone lion
guards the entrance
to Chinatown

As voting rights and citizenship were gradually extended, the Chinese increasingly left their enclave with its mah jong parlours and old-world introspection and became assimilated into the larger society. By the 1950s, Victoria's Chinatown had become a shadow. Luckily, a recent multi-million dollar revivification program has brought renewed colour and energy. Highlighted by the wonderful Gate of Harmonious Interest, which stands more than 11 metres tall and spans Fisgard Street, Chinatown proudly welcomes visitors to stroll through the bustling markets that spill out onto the sidewalk, to investigate the vibrant shops filled with exotic art and crafts, and to sample the cuisine that wafts aromatically through the air from the numerous chow mein and noodle houses lining Fisgard Street.

Although they have little reason to be grateful for the grudging welcome and exploitative treatment that were meted out to the first generations, the current Chinese-Canadians can take great satisfaction in their unique contributions, which have added immeasurable vitality and charm to Victoria.

Right at the corner of Fisgard and Government, where the

massive Gate of Harmonious Interest marks where Chinatown officially begins, look for **Eastern Interiors** (572 Fisgard Street, 385-4643), which sells bonsai, various ceramics, floral wall scrolls, and jewellery. Their classic cloisonné vases — in characteristic blue — are several hundred dollars. Souvenir seekers can pick up jade figurines, beads, earrings, and mini-Buddhas for $5. **Magpie** (556 Fisgard Street, 383-1880) sells Asian antiques, sculpture, wall hangings, Japanese woodblock prints, and elegant jewellery carved from amber and jade. And you'll have fun in **Chinatown Trading Company** (551 Fisgard Street, 381-5503): even if some of the knick-knacks are deliberately corny, the profusion of stuff in this series of three connected shops creates a bazaar-like atmosphere that helps recapture the fabled "mystery of the East." They sell colourful fans, sake sets, those ubiquitous woven baskets (some big enough to be hope chests), bamboo flutes, origami kits, fancy ceramic candlestick holders, kites, and even gear like oven-proofed scallop shells on which to serve up your latest seafood recipes. There are a few different mini-historical displays and tableaux (look for the glass case containing the stunning emperor's dragon robe), and they sell lots of silly little things for $2 or $3. Probably the most interesting shop is **Fan Tan Gallery** (541 Fisgard Street, 382-4424), which resembles a United Nations of folk art due to its proliferation of gorgeous and unusual imports such as Peruvian tribal pottery and African masks. It also sells colourful kitchen gear, wicker baskets, candles, and nifty knick-knacks.

Halfway down Fisgard is **Fan Tan Alley**, a narrow corridor that connects through to Pandora Avenue. This is Canada's narrowest street, and even though Fan Tan Alley has lost much of its Chinese character, it is a perfect microcosom of the "bohemian" resettlement that took place downtown during the seventies as artists and other anti-suburbanites took advantage of cheap rents. Contained in Fan Tan are hip little boutiques selling collectable records (**The Turntable,** 107-3, 382-5543), runes and palmistry (**Triple Spiral,** 106-3, 380-7212), as well as coffee bars, barber shops, and other amenities. No trip to Victoria is complete without an amble through the alley!

And situated near the outskirts of Chinatown are a few other shops that are well worth a visit. **Lido** (101-1619 Store Street,

Fan Tan Alley, the
narrowest street in
Canada, holds the
secret to Chinatown

480-0589) flaunts a hiply retro sensibility, selling kitsch-plus
collectables from the forties to the sixties. The owner travels as
far as Portland to unearth everything from vintage clothing to
Jetsons-style flying V coffee tables. And just down the street
don't miss **Capital Iron** (1900 Store Street, 385-9703), which
started business about 75 years ago as a few sheds that were
fronted by a junk pile of discards. At some point it became a
more civilized hardware store, but Capital Iron has long since
outgrown that function and become a Victoria institution. While
its two buildings house everything from hammers to hiking
boots, the heart of the store is the "collectables" area in the
basement. This browser's haven has commando clothing, gas
masks, exit signs, whalers' scrimshaw, MP helmets, weird
gizmos, and exotic marine antiques like a ship's wheel and
mount. Few businesses in Victoria boast as much character or
history as Capital Iron.

Chintz & Company
1720 Store Street   *381-2404*

For anyone who hasn't taken a vow of poverty, this celebration of beautiful living could put a serious strain on the old MasterCard. Chintz is a cornucopia of everything from Italian dinnerwear, carved wooden chairs, and terracotta garden pieces to metalwork, furniture, textiles, vases, and Spanish glassware. Their cloth and wooden flowers (huge cloth onions, giant hollyhocks and roses, etc.) could make anyone into an interior designer. Chintz offers many unique items of unusual beauty and quality.

ANTIQUE ROW

Victoria is known around North America as a great spot to search for quality antiques, particularly those of British origin. Because of the city's special links with England, and also due to its status as a pre-eminent retirement centre, Victoria has always attracted citizens who own exceptional collections of porcelain, furniture, silver, and objêts d'art. Regular "estate sales" keep a steady supply of Georgian candlesticks and Chippendale chairs moving through the city's numerous antique stores. Located mostly on three blocks of Fort Street — the merchants themselves paid to have the street signs altered to read "Antique Row" — these shops offer an opportunity to browse through three centuries of literal treasures. Although some of the stores stock collectables and "junque" more than actual antiques, they're all worth at least a quick browse. (And keep in mind that antiques certified at over 100 years of age are duty free.)

Going from west to east, the best shops include: **Pacific Antiques** (805 Fort, 388-5311), specializing in eighteenth- and nineteenth-century furniture, china, silver, and glass; **Romanoff & Company** (837 Fort, 480-1543), elegantly displaying everything from ancient coins and Oriental pieces to art glass and estate jewellery; and **Domus Antica** (1038/40 Fort, 385-5443), which offers furniture (particularly English), porcelain, glass, pewter, and paintings. Collectors who take a shine to silver shouldn't miss **Jeffries & Co. Silversmiths** (1026 Fort, 383-8315).

One of Victoria's best shops is **David Robinson Ltd.** (1023 Fort, 384-6425), displaying a choice selection of furniture, Oriental rugs, silver, porcelain, brass, and other collectables. Furniture fans shouldn't miss taking a look in **Charles Baird**

Antiques (1044A Fort, 384-8809), which boasts many fine and unusual pieces. And don't overlook **Wendy Russell Antiques** (525 Fort, 385-9816), which is a few blocks off Antique Row. Wendy Russell has an eye for beauty: she specializes in estate and antique jewellry and small objêts d'art, including some wonderful Japanese and Chinese pieces.

Saving the best for last we have **Faith Grant** (1156 Fort, 383-0121). Even after her death in 1985, Faith Grant still seems to be the benign matriarch of Victoria's antique shops. As the shop that bears her name enters its eighth decade, currently under the stewardship of grandchildren Heather Graham-Dickson and Forrest Graham, it offers a fascinating opportunity for collectors to step into the past. An authentic heritage setting — this 1862 building is one of the oldest surviving structures in the city — Faith Grant boasts 18 rooms and 1,950 square metres devoted to a general collection of silver, furnishings, pictures, and brass. Aside from complete sets of hallmarked English flatware, you can typically find exceptional furniture: perhaps an early-nineteenth-century breakfront bookcase in satinwood or maybe a "key wind" dining room table from the Victorian era. Ask to visit the "box room," which is filled with tea caddies, jewel boxes, and lap boxes (portable desks used to write letters whilst travelling in your carriage) made of walnut, mahogany, or rosewood.

A few noteworthy shops with more contemporary interests include **Caspian Persian Carpets** (825 Fort, 383-3434), which specializes in Persian rugs and has Victoria's best selection. Bibliophiles can browse in either **Wells Books** (832 Fort, 360-2929) or **Vintage Books** (839 Fort, 382-4414). And don't overlook **The Museum Shop** (1011 Fort, 381-5553), one of the most interesting stores in the city. Nearly unique in the world — most "museum shops" are set in specific art museums and just sell replicas from their own collections — it stocks treasures from around the globe. Its jewellery, including scarab earrings and gold-finished florin cufflinks, is definitely eye- catching. The shelves also offer Greek statues, cards and address books, Chinese horses, and Egyptian ankh candle holders. Prices are surprisingly modest: the most expensive things for sale are the Gothic monkey trolls from Notre Dame Cathedral and furniture painted with reproductions of work by artists like Frida Kahlo

and Monet. An information card is supplied with each reproduction, but you don't have to be a scholar to shop here!

DOWNTOWN

"Downtown" Victoria is an area by default: it is what's left over
after all the more identifiable portions have asserted their distinct
identities on our informal map. The listings begin at the Empress
Hotel and the adjoining Conference Centre. We then continue up
Victoria's central avenue, Douglas Street, en route to some interesting side-street shopping.

While visiting the Empress, don't overlook the **Art of Man
Gallery** (383-3800). This superb gallery of Canadian Indian
and Inuit art is a must-see, although I suspect that only connoisseur collectors with spare bullion in the bank will be the
major customers. The seven linguistic groups of the Northwest
Coast are all represented, as are some of the Plains Indians
such as the Cree and Ojibway. Pieces range from masks and
carved moose horn to Inuit prints and rattles and headdresses;
prices are steep, topping $15,000 for, say, an exquisite Haida
argillite box.

G. Gagliano of Florence
750 Douglas Street *361-3344*

Leather lovers beware, this place stocks superb merchandise.
The owner, an expatriate Florentine, handles mostly leathers
and clothing imported directly from Italy. A gifted designer
himself (he supplies to clients like Saks in New York), Mr.
Gagliano augments his own unique handbags, shoes, briefcases,
and sweaters with gorgeous silk scarves, knitwear, ties, and
jewellery. But his men's and women's jackets are probably the
show-stealers. Made from expertly tanned lambskin that feels
as soft as cashmere, these ultra-luxury garments are priced at
$600 to $2,000.

Stephen Lowe Art Gallery
752 Douglas Street *384-3912*

A superb gallery of Oriental art. See "*Art Galleries*" in **Arts and
Entertainment**.

Harry Roet at Pop
Culture: "If you
don't need it, we
have it!"
(*jackie garrow*)

   Sunday's Snowflakes (1000 Douglas Street, 381-4461) is
a women's clothing store that has regularly been voted the finest
in the city in *Monday Magazine*'s best-of annual poll. They
feature exclusively Canadian designers, make a point of carrying small sizes, and pride themselves on personal service. Almost all of their fabrics are naturals like cottons, wools, and
silks; their jewellery and accessories are typically handmade.
Prices generally are upper-moderate. The brightest retail light
in the recently renovated Sussex Place (corner of Douglas and
Broughton Street) is **Pop Culture** (G-9, 386-8280), a zesty
celebration of all that's silly and ephemeral. Their stock ranges
from miniature patio lights tricked out as plastic fruit, retro
fridge magnets, oddball ties, goofy inflatable toys, and mini
lava lamps to hiply rude T-shirts and even the occasional
upmarket item like glass artworks. The store more than lives
up to the owner's motto: "If you don't need it, we have it!"
   Bernard Callebaut (623 Broughton Street, 380-1515) is a
fourth-generation chocolate maker, and he's done his Belgian
forebears proud. Bernard uses only the finest grade of Belgian
chocolate, and his elegant confections are flavoured with li-
queurs and cognacs, marzipan, mocha, pralines, ginger, and cara-
mel. He also has gold- and silver-coated chocolates, five delicate
crème fraîche delights, and hazelnut ice cream bars. Different
sins of the flesh are catered to at **Curves** (1002 Broad Street,
381-6112). Whether you want to be triumphantly slinky in a
silken camisole or clad in a more virtuous flannel nightie, this
shop can make your bedtime appearance naughty or nice … and
in the best of taste. Their nightwear is typically sheer and elegant,

in lush colours (but there are some lavender long johns for women who prefer to heat up themselves instead of their partner).

Roots (1010 Broad Street, 383-4811) is an all-Canadian store that has turned the beaver into an international symbol of shopping goodwill: cosmopolitan shoppers come here in droves to pick up those signature sweatshirts and T-shirts. Roots clothing is made from exceptionally fine leather, and their big-seller jackets and bags last for a long time (jackets are made from a full hide of leather). Their shoes are attractive and also waterproof. And next door at **Bustopher Jones** (1012 Broad Street, 388-6628), fashion is friendly and with a hint of youthful exuberance: the wide-ranging selection of women's clothes favours the Esprit and Mexx end of the spectrum. Aside from slightly dressier skirts and blouses they have a *sportif* line featuring the colourful togs of Vuarnet and Mistral. **Benetton** (1015 Broad Street, 384-0300) has turned its Italian clothing line for men and women into a world-wide empire by offering dressily casual active wear at affordable prices. Benetton features mostly Italian knitwear; the tops, sweaters, jeans, pants, and skirts are typically pure cotton or wool. Benetton's "European" look emphasizes vibrant colours and an easy-going sense of coordination.

Wine lovers shouldn't miss out on **The Wine Barrel** (644 Broughton Street, 388-0606), which boasts Reidel glassware, gourmet foods (including wine-flavoured jams), professional corkscrews, wine accessories such as T-shirts and humorous cards, and an extensive library. While not actually selling wine yet, they are working on obtaining a licence. **Scaramouche** (635 Fort Street, 386-2215) is a gentle store that seems like a scented, charming ramble through the past. Scaramouche specializes in Canadian folk art, but they have exotic kitchen favours (jams, chutneys, and preserves); handmade pine furniture, featuring tongue-and-groove construction; and a potpourri of stuff like pottery, throw pillows, scented candles, woven wreaths, braided rugs, brass bird cages, soaps, and scents. Don't overlook their excellent selection of antique reproduction jewellery ($10-$150).

Crabtree & Evelyn
640 Fort Street   *388-0102*

If you want to gentrify your lifestyle, take an aromatic stroll through Canada's orignal Crabtree store. Their gleaming mahogany shelves are brimming with English and Swiss soaps, bath beads, and room fragrances; sybaritic shaving gear (up to $115 for a shaving brush with silver-tipped badger bristles); and elegant gift boxes and cards. And don't overlook their array of "comestibles" from England and France: they have a diet-destroying cornucopia of taste treats such as liqueur jams, spiced mustards, cheese biscuits, almond shortbread, and blackcurrant chocolate crisps.

Alcheringa
665 Fort Street   *383-8224*

Years ago it sold Australian and New Zealand imports and had art as a sideline; today it is Victoria's second great store for connoisseurs of aboriginal art. Featuring work from Papua New Guinea, Australia, and the Pacific Northwest, Alcheringa looks like a museum (and carries work of that calibre). Most of what they sell goes to collectors in California and New York, but some people do walk in off the street and spend $16,000 for a totem pole or $8,000 for a Walter Harris tribal mask. They also sell silkscreens, painted paddles, didgeridoos, and silver jewellery.

"Casual European elegance" is the theme at **Baden-Baden** (611 Fort Street, 380-1063), a women's clothing store that stocks exclusively West German designs, featuring well-made and interesting fabrics. Aside from their 100 percent silks and fabrics, they stock viscose and other easy-care fabrics such as a convincing synthetic "leather" that's washable. Baden-Baden deals exclusively in separates, and prices are upper moderate. Casual with a hint of class is the outlook at **Outlooks For Men** (1231 Broad Street, 384-6121), one of Victoria's more distinctive and reliable sources for decent clothing options for guys with self-respect. **Kitchen Charisma** (714 View Street, 384-8823) caters to both the kitchen and bathroom and has lots of unusual items: Portuguese ceramics, interesting cookbooks, functional gear, and objêts d'art. **T.J.'s Decorative Art** (716 View Street, 480-4930) features marine artifacts, Northwest Coast and Asian art, Henry Hunt totems, and various antiques. Worth a peek to the serious collector. And if you're running out of books to read, the upstairs portion of **Russell Books** (743 Fort Street, 361-4447) has over 20,000 used tomes to choose from.

Music lovers will applaud **A & B Sound** (641 Yates Street, 385-1461) which, with ready access to over 100,000 titles, has one of the better selections of CDs and tapes in North America. The rock and pop section is typically jammed with teens buying the latest by Hole and Smashing Pumpkins; a more restful adjoining area houses about an acre of classical and jazz discs. And serious music buffs always include **Endangered Species** (1315 Douglas Street, 360-0098) on their shopping sprees: the selection isn't huge, but chances are that this is the only shop in town that will be carrying the latest releases not making it on the radio playlists (e.g., hip jazz, blues, and folk artists such as Bill Frissell, Joe Ely, Jerry Douglas, and Peter Case). Also worth your time is **Lyle's Place** (726 Yates Street, 382-8422), the largest of Victoria's "alternative" record stores. As well as a huge expanse of new and used records and CDs (including rare sets and collector's items), they also do a big trade in music paraphernalia such as posters, calendars, and T-shirts.

The English Sweet Shoppe
738 Yates Street   *382-3325*

A Victoria institution for three-quarters of a century, the English Sweet Shoppe has always been a mecca for the city's greedily grateful sweet tooths. Alongside those rows of glass jars brimming with conventional treats like jubes and licorice kids, they stock such venerable pleasures as Callard & Bowser toffees, Everton mints, Faulder's floral gums, Terry's chocolate oranges, and the authentic English Cadbury's. They also sell a classic opera roll, which has a nougatine centre rolled in assorted nuts.

ARTS AND ENTERTAINMENT

THE ARTS

Despite Victoria's tourist image as a quaint little spot tucked into a corner of the land of mountains and Mounties, the cultural life here is vivid, varied, and surprisingly contemporary. This beautiful city has attracted a disproportionately large number of artists, musicians, and performers and the arts scene is subsequently lively and full of colour. Whether your passion is opera or old-timey music, modern dance or live drama, Victoria can engage your heart and mind.

The nightlife scene is equally sophisticated, ranging from intimate lounges and bohemian bistros to elegant discos and rock and jazz clubs that bring in artists as diverse as B.B. King and Ani Di Franco.

The most useful guide to what's on in Victoria can be found in *Monday Magazine*, a free local weekly (it's distributed widely throughout downtown: look for its bright yellow display boxes). *Monday*'s comprehensive calendar listings cover everything from bake sales to Bach oratorios.

Tickets for major cultural events are on sale through either Tourism Victoria in the Inner Harbour (953-2033) or the McPherson Box Office, corner of Government Street and Pandora Avenue (386-6121).

THEATRE

Unfortunately, theatre season and tourist scene don't overlap much — but if you are here during the fall or winter, do check out what's on at **The Belfry** (1291 Gladstone Avenue, 385-6815), our leading professional theatrical company, or **Intrepid Theatre** (383-2663), which offers an eclectic mix of alternative theatrical fare.

Our **Shakespeare Festival** runs for several weeks in July and August, sited in a huge tent right down at the Inner Harbour. This features performances by several different local troupes and is definitely a must-see. Equally English, but less high-toned, are **Capitol City Comedy**'s British farces that run annually in July and August; these often showcase our best local actors, and are surprisingly nimble entertainments (386-6121). And the summer is always capped in late August by the **Fringe Festival** (383-2663), which for more than a decade has boasted a genuine crazy-quilt of alternative theatre: six venues run simultaneously, and the offerings range from stark versions of Shakespeare tragedies to new-wave vaudeville, from multi-media dance performances to musical cabaret. Performers come from all over the world, piggy-backing their way from one Fringe to the next. If you've never been, don't hesitate: tickets are cheap and the sense of pleasure and discovery is alarmingly invigorating!

MUSIC

Again, due to timing, most tourists won't be able to take advantage of what is probably Victoria's best cultural group: **Pacific Opera Victoria** (385-0222), which has earned a national reputation for its innovative performances. You'll have better luck with the **Victoria Symphony** (385-6515), which is one of the finer symphonies in Canada; although their regular season is fall-winter, they put on an extensive program of summer concerts, culminating in Symphony Splash, an outdoor performance on the first Sunday in August at the Inner Harbour that attracts up to 50,000 listeners.

Some of the music festivals to note are the **TerrifVic Dixieland Jazz Party** (953-2011), which occurs in the third week in April and attracts dozens of the world's best dixieland bands. A more progressive tone is struck by **JazzFest** (388-4423), which runs for 10 days at the end of June and features a smorgasbord of jazz, blues, worldbeat, and gospel. (This event attracts stars such as McCoy Tyner, Joe Lovano, the Blind Boys of Alabama, and Otis Rush.)

If you like your classical music in a bucolic setting, then **Eine Kleine Summer Music** (382-1158) should be your cup

The Shinto shrine is one of many treasures at the Art Gallery of Greater Victoria

of Mozart. Set in a small hall on the pastoral Saanich Peninsula, this fine ensemble puts on a six-week season of Sunday after-noon concerts that are fun and friendly. The repertoire favours the Classical and Romantic periods, and the pieces could be anything from a sonata duo up to a quintet.

Debuting in 1996, the **Victoria Summer Music Festival** (382-3803) is a concert series of classical chamber music rang-ing from baroque to Bartok, featuring our best local musicians in combination with select international guests.

ART GALLERIES

Art Gallery of Greater Victoria
1040 Moss Street   *384-4101*

The AGGV, Victoria's premier art venue, is considered one of the better "little" galleries in North America. Sited in the turn-of-the-century Spencer Mansion, this historically oriented gallery has more than 10,000 pieces in its permanent collec-tion. Although the six exhibition rooms show everything from the finest contemporary Canadian art to, say, travelling exhibi-tions on medieval manuscripts, the AGGV is most famed for its outstanding collection of Asian art — the Japanese collec-tion is quite simply the best in the country. After taking the indoor tour, by no means overlook the Japanese garden, the centrepiece of which is the only Shinto shrine in existence outside Japan.

Fran Willis North Park Gallery
1619 Store Street   *381-3422*

With those soaring white walls and the huge, semi-circular windows letting in a ton of light, this is one beautiful gallery. Fran Willis runs things with taste and imagination, and she features a strong representation of contemporary art — oils, mixed media, bronzes — by B.C. and Alberta artists. Ceramics and raku are also displayed here.

Open Space
510 Fort Street   *383-8833*

This artist-run gallery has, with self-confidence (and a few dashes of pretension), been a major definer of the avant-garde in Victoria since 1971. Although the art shows range from cutting-edge work from North America's larger centres to representations by this area's finest artists, Open Space has also embraced music, dance, and theatre as part of its mandate.

Stephen Lowe Gallery
752 Douglas Street   *384-3912*

Stephen Lowe was one of this century's greatest Chinese artists. Although he studied at the traditional Lingnan School in China, after he emigrated to Canada Lowe developed a unique hybrid of Chinese tradition and Western technique. He and Eunice established their own gallery in his new hometown of Victoria in 1972; Lowe's tragically early death in 1975 turned the shop into something of a shrine. When 130 of Lowe's delicately poetic watercolours toured China in 1985, they provoked about as much sensation as the Rolling Stones.

Today, while the gallery still memorializes Lowe by selling his limited-edition framed prints, it also stocks a unique and gorgeous selection of rare antiques and fine art from the Orient. It has Chinese carving in jade, rose quartz, and lapis lazuli; Qing "tapestries" taken from the sleeves and backs of 100-year-old garments; and a fine selection of monochrome-glazed porcelain from China, including *sang-de-boeuf* and amber crackle. It also sells hand-moulded Tang Dynasty reproductions.

West End Gallery
1203 Broad Street   *388-0009*

This small and tasteful gallery features original art from some
of Canada's best artists, both established and emerging. There
are a lot of oil paintings (mostly representational — look for
the Quebec landscapes), plus some whimsical ceramics and a
few multi-media pieces that probably wouldn't fit easily into
your luggage.

Winchester Galleries
1545 Fort Street   *595-2777*

Any serious collectors of contemporary painting should drop
into this gallery at Oak Bay Junction: the walls are densely
covered with work from the area's most gifted artists, including Jack Wilkinson, Herbert Siebner, Anthony Thorn, and
Myfanwy Pavelic, who is probably Canada's most famous por-
traitist. The owners love art and the people who make it; drop in
and share your passion with them. Prices range from several
hundred dollars for a modest West Coast watercolour to 10
times that for an oil painting that will provide much inspiration
for metaphysical musing.

NIGHTLIFE

Live Music

The Limit
1318 Broad Street   *384-3557*

Victoria's hippest venue for live music, favouring indie acts
and name-brands from the Canadian and American alternative
college rock scene. Mondays and Tuesdays it's canned music,
but the DJs know what they're doing.

The Planet
15 Bastion Square   *385-5333*

This venerable club used to be *the* place to go for live music in
Victoria. But a sluggish economy has forced retrenchment: now
it alternates a house band with predictably hip canned music.
Tasteful decor and plush furniture attract Gen-Xers who wish
they were yuppies.

Legends
919 Douglas Street 383-7137

After a $500,000 reno in the winter of 1996, this once-disheveled club has transformed from pit to palace. Even better, they've also hired Victoria's most experienced music booker, who brings in sophisticated international fare including Afro-pop, R&B, jazz, and blues.

Hermann's Jazz Club
753 View Street 388-9166

This is a fine, straight-ahead jazz joint. The walls are too darned red to call the place beautiful, but the acoustics are better than most, the food's good, there's decent beer on tap, and the music gets treated with respect. Guest stars such as Sheila Jordan and David Murray have gigged here, but Hermann's typically features mainstream players from Victoria, Vancouver, and the Pacific Northwest.

McMorran's Restaurant
5109 Cordova Bay Road 658-5224

Now here's a real treasure! In operation for more than 60 years, McMorran's features dress-code dancing every Saturday night out on the maple floor of the Seaview Room, where they bring in various big bands to celebrate the long-gone elegance of Glenn Miller, Jimmy Dorsey, and the other stars of the swing era. The pre-dance dinner is optional.

Steamers
570 Yates Street 381-4340

What used to be one of downtown's grubbier peeler parlours got a total facelift and was reborn as a first-rate blues bar. Aside from pulling in the best blues artists from the Northwest, they also feature occasional forays into Celtic, folk, and worldbeat music.

Vertigo
Student Union Building, UVic 721-8355

Sited at the University of Victoria, Vertigo is run by the same entrepreneurs behind The Limit (see above) and features a similar emphasis on alternative/college bands, but with more of a dance-friendly attitude.

Recorded Music

The Drawing Room
751 View Street   *920-7797*

With the same owners as The Planet (see above), this is another plush hang-out for "hip" lounge lizards who smoke the occasional Cuban cigar while striking an upmarket Gen-X pose. Music includes hip-hop, funk, and retro-rock.

Scandals
770 Yates Street   *389-0666*

The fading star of the not-quite-mainstream recorded music scene. Attracts a college crowd and is passably hip.

Uforia
1208 Wharf Street   *381-2331*

An under-30 crowd comes here, looking for basic Top-40 dance music that will inspire equally basic thoughts in someone they hope to meet, after a few tequila shooters.

Sweetwaters
Market Square   *383-7844*

This elegant and ever-popular singles bar features classic Motown to the latest dance-happy hits. Attracts a middle-of-the-road, late-'20s to mid-'40s crowd.

BILLIARDS

People who take their social cue from slate and green velvet can choose among several joints where billiards could be mistaken for a religion: **Cues on View** (708 View Street, 480-7789); **Red Rock City** (1630 Store Street, 388-0836); **Peacock Billiards** (834 Johnson Street, 384-3332).

COCKTAILS FOR TWO … SSSH!

Bengal Room (Empress Hotel)
721 Government Street   *384-8111*

The lounge in the stunningly renovated Empress Hotel celebrates the India of Imperial Britain. From tiger skins and sandalwood screens to wall-length murals and huge kneeling elephants carved out of ebony, the Bengal Room confidently

The Empress Hotel's
exquisitely cosy
Bengal Room

asserts the pluck and pretense of mutton-chop England. Care for
a gin and tonic, old chap? Definitely a must-see.

Lobby Lounge (Harbour Towers)
345 Quebec Street 385-2405

Comfortable elegance is what this lobby lounge is all about:
the divider walls are fashioned out of those wrinkly glass tiles
and the room has the sinuous curves and recesses of the moderne
style. Occasional piano music to go along with that ever-so-
dry martini.

Trophy's (Hotel Grand Pacific)
450 Quebec Street 386-0450

This is one of Victoria's newer posh hotels and it has an appropriately spiffy lounge, Trophy's. It's all wool carpets, dim lights,
brass, chandeliers, dark wood, pianos, and a classy big-TV in-
stallation for Armani-suited sports buffs. Nice atmosphere, and
it's rarely crowded. A patio with somewhat more casual chairs
overlooks the glassed-in 25-metre pool.

Cook's Landing (Laurel Point)
680 Montreal Street					386-8721

Dreamy sea views, well-crafted cocktails, and languid lounge pianistics are on the menu at the classy Cook's Landing lounge.

Rick's Lounge (Ocean Pointe Resort)
45 Songhees Road					360-2999

Casual elegance is the theme in Rick's Lounge, where you can listen to piano music while reclining in comfy chairs with commanding water views of the Inner Harbour. After polishing off that snifter of Courvoisier, say hello to Saffron, the friendly ring-necked parakeet in the adjoining lobby.

The Snug (Oak Bay Beach Hotel)
1175 Beach Drive					598-4556

Holding court in Oak Bay's heartland, in the Tudor-style elegance of the Oak Bay Beach Hotel, is one of Victoria's most venerable bars. It's only a few kilometres from the university, and duffle-coated students and their slightly tweedier profs join the other well-dressed patrons when they need some beaujolais to bring some colour back to their cheeks after that two-hour lecture on the semiotics of Jane Austen. There are sea views, and the excellent pub fare tastes even better out on the balcony.

LIVELIER LIBATIONS

Bartholomew's
777 Douglas Street					389-5111

Set right downtown in the Executive House, this turn-of-the-century-style bar features dark wood, ceiling fans, Tiffany lamps, old-timey sports photos, and stained glass in the ceiling. The bar gets pretty noisy with the sounds of a full house of exuberant patrons. And if you're in a less celebratory mood, stroll down the hall to Doubles, Executive House's sedate and elegant oyster bar. Even if you don't want to get intimate with a bivalve, the coffered ceilings, leather sofas, and dark wood panelling go well with a cocktail or two.

The Bayside Lounge
455 Belleville Street					386-2421

Located in the Quality Inn Harbourview (formerly The Crest

Hotel), this is a sleekly appointed and splendidly sited lounge with second-storey views of the Inner Harbour. The Bayside Lounge is well worth a drop-in after you've been shopping for kilts and totem poles all day.

Big Bad John's
919 Douglas Street   *383-7137*

Welcome to Victoria's only "hillbilly bar," complete with plank floors and a prankster bartender who'll drop a plastic spider via a string when you're least expecting it. Head for the Strathcona Hotel if you want casual camaraderie and the chance to get a bit rowdy, 'cause this here's the spot for y'all.

Cuckoo's Nest
919 Douglas Street   *383-7137*

Tucked into the Strathcona Hotel is the Cuckoo's Nest, a hip sports bar decked out in dark wood and Tiffany lamps. The music ranges from Top 40 to the latest hits off the college radio circuit, except when the big-screen TV pulls in satellite sports.

Hunter's
759 Yates Street   *384-7494*

This funkily elegant restaurant/tapas bar/lounge attracts a lively younger crowd. After 10 PM it's one of the busiest bars in town. And downstairs there's Triples, a small sports bar complete with TV and pool tables.

Swiftsure Lounge
427 Belleville Street   *386-3451*

Located in the Days Inn on the Harbour, the Swiftsure Lounge has long since dumped its kitschy nautical look in favour of copper, dark wicker, and recessed ceiling ovals. You can order sushi or wine by the glass while taking in attractive views of the boats bobbing in front of the downtown skyline.

PUBS

Christie's Carriage House
1739 Fort Street   *598-5333*

Here's a fancy yet still comfortable neighbourhood pub, finished in high-Edwardian fashion with brass lamps, stained glass, dark woods, and wallpaper striped like a banker's shirt.

Christie's is a handsomely restored heritage building, a fine example of Queen Anne-style architecture. This deservedly popular watering hole features a variety of handmade drafts on tap.

Garrick's Head Pub
69 Bastion Square   *384-6835*

Neither over-decorated nor over-cute, this is one of the more
authentic-feeling "English" pubs in the city. Oak beams, an
unvarnished wood floor, and a formidable wood bar help re-
call the spirit of the original Garrick, which was built in 1867.
The current version has the usual bottled beer plus three fine
drafts brewed locally by Vancouver Island Brewery and served
in authentic "sleeves"; try the delicious dark lager, which is
named in honour of Hermann the brewmaster. And they even
have real pretzels.

Spinnakers
308 Catherine Street   *386-2739*

This has to be one of the best pubs in North America. With an
on-site micro-brewery that makes some of Canada's finest ale,
bitters, and stout, great views across Lime Bay towards the
Inner Harbour and the Legislature, dart boards and varied
evening entertainment, and fine "pub grub" well worth stick-
ing a fork into, Spinnakers can encourage you to stretch "just
one" into a full evening's pleasure.

Sticky Wicket
919 Douglas Street   *383-7137*

A $4-million renovation to the Strathcona Hotel resulted in no
less than five separate bars at this address. Whether you want
to sip British beer at the elegant "Irish Bar" or take the elevator
up to the roof for rum punch under a sun umbrella, the Sticky
Wicket will slake your thirst in fine style. The kitchen dishes
up some fine meals, so don't be in a hurry to leave!

Swans
506 Pandora Avenue   *361-3310*

Downtown Victoria's best pub by far is Swans, an attractively
old-fashioned watering hole that's been busy since the day it
opened. Swans is an exceptionally fine brewpub, and its
made-on-site beers and ales, which contain all-natural ingredients and are brewed British-style, are all worth appreciating.

The food is very good as well. And the owner of Swans is a genuine art connoisseur: there is better original art on the walls here than you'll find in most of the city's galleries.

GAY CLUBS

Rumors Cabaret
1325 Government Street 385-0566

Welcome to Victoria's premier gay club, "the place where the women shoot pool and the men dance," according to one cheeky habitué. And that large dance floor gets more than full on the weekends. Rumors attracts a generally younger crowd, and the music is hot.

GARDENS AND PARKS

Although much of the "Englishness" in Victoria is little more than a cute fraud which has, through countless repetition, convinced even the locals of its authenticity, our British passion for gardens and parks is surpassingly genuine. Right from Victoria's earliest days, when the area's first plutocrats were erecting massive estates with grandiose titles like *Ashnola* and *Burleith*, elegant landscaping was considered an essential; aside from mimicking the grand manners of the motherland, it was a dramatic way of taming a raw and new environment.

Today, those initial endeavours have themselves engendered a harvest of private and public gardens and parks that is the envy of the country. Blessed with a temperate climate, Victoria marks the slow wheeling of the seasons starting with the pink-smudged tree blossoms that herald the coming rainbow blooms of late spring and summer.

But it is principally owing to an enthusiastic army of amateur gardeners that Victoria boasts the thousands of floral displays that are the marvel of visitors. There are many specialized horticultural groups in the city — with interests ranging from alpine plants to exotic rhododendrons — and their efforts have achieved such renown that sister groups from as far away as Oregon come here on charter bus tours to admire their colourful handiwork.

URBAN PARKS AND GARDENS

Beacon Hill Park
Named for a double set of beacon fires that were lit as a navigational aid in decades gone by, Beacon Hill Park provides one of Victoria's most pleasant outings. Its 75 hectares include expanses of assiduously cultivated gardens (30,000 annuals

More than 700,000 visitors a year come to marvel at Butchart Gardens
(*Butchart Gardens Ltd.*)

are planted twice yearly), rustic stone bridges, numerous duck
ponds, and a stately aquatic facility for the haughty resident
swans. There is also a petting zoo, playing fields where
whites-wearing cricketeers pursue their arcane pleasures, towering evergreens, and a few shady bowers offering respite when
the summer heat comes radiating off the nearby city streets.
Roses are a big thing here, and the two best displays are near
the cricket pitch on the east side and close by the children's
wading pool to the west.

All that luxurious landscaping gives way to more natural
rhythms where the south-facing portion of the park rolls down
towards Dallas Road and the waters of the Strait of Juan de
Fuca. More than 100,000 daffodils are scattered in gay yellow
clumps along these slopes (don't dare pick them!). Benches
offer views out to sea, and they're also a nice vantage point
from which to watch joggers, bicyclists, and the occasional
hang gliders catching the updrafts from the steep Dallas Road
cliffs. Paths lead down to the pebbly, log-strewn oceanfront,
which offers a fine beachcombing stroll.

Butchart Gardens
800 Benvenuto Drive   652-5256

Here is Victoria's single most outstanding tourist attraction,
known around the globe. Built out of an abandoned limestone
quarry, Butchart's 20 hectares are a lush celebration of horticultural beauty; here's undeniable — and aromatic! — proof
that gardening truly is an art form. (See **Sightseeing** for a full
description.)

Government House
1401 Rockland Avenue   387-2080

Although this Rockland mansion houses the Lieutenant- Governor — the Queen's representative to provincial government
— the exquisitely maintained gardens and grounds are anything but a state secret: many of Victoria's brides get their wedding photos taken in this beautiful setting. Visitors are not permitted
to enter the building, but are welcome to stroll the grounds when-
ever the gate is open, typically from dawn to dusk. One of
Victoria's most interesting civic projects has been the volunteer
efforts of literally hundreds of gardeners who have laboured to
reclaim and expand the original gardens. Although the gorgeous,
sweet-smelling roses are particularly prized, don't overlook the
expanse of "wild" meadow garden that comprises various native
flowers and grasses plus one of Victoria's few remaining thick-
ets of Garry oak. (And consider taking a drive up peculiar
Lotbiniere Avenue, the narrow, rock wall-lined street that flanks
the Government House property to the west.)

Horticultural Centre of the Pacific
505 Quayle Road   479-6162

Gardeners have to get their start somewhere, and this special
"teaching garden" has 44 hectares that include roses, shade
plants, a winter garden (yes, it's true!), and a fuchsia and be-
gonia arbour that is a phenomenal blaze of colour. As befits its
educational mandate, more humble vegetable and fruit tree
plantings are incorporated into the Centre, which runs an ongoing series of seasonal weekend workshops. Not too hard to
find, the Centre is about 15 minutes from downtown: from Pat
Bay Highway get onto West Saanich Road, turn west onto Beaver Lake Road and follow it to where it intersects Quayle Road.

Royal Roads University
2005 Sooke Road   *391-2511*

Dating from 1908, and originally a 260-hectare estate owned by coal heir James Dunsmuir (whose father built Craigdarroch Castle), Royal Roads was commissioned during the Second World War and latterly served as a military college. The main building is the perfectly grand Hatley Castle, which was built so that James Dunsmuir could have a baronial backdrop for his parties. Dunsmuir is rumoured to have commissioned renowned local architect Samuel Maclure with the words "Money doesn't matter, just build what I want." The bill came to around $1 million. Its spacious grounds, which unfold at a gentle incline towards Esquimalt Lagoon, house a Japanese garden, whose subtle ceremonial character embraces evocative pools and a floating teahouse; an Italian garden, passionate despite its strict formality; and a handsome rose garden. Victoria's mania for floral displays was undoubtedly subverting even this military college: maybe that's why the federal government court-martialled it in 1994; the decommissioned buildings have now been converted into a university. The gardens are free and open to the public daily from dawn till dusk. Royal Roads is easy to spot: look for a long, two-metre fence on Sooke Road, about 16 kilometres west of Victoria.

Saxe Point Park
Here's a fine park little-known to many Victorians. Overlooking the water and offering fine sea views across the Strait of Juan de Fuca to Washington State's Olympic Mountains, Saxe Point combines formally cultivated gardens with natural woodland. When you've finished that picnic lunch, or want to cool off after having a hackysack workout on the grass, take a cooling stroll through the woodsy trails. Beachcombers can ply their trade here (and you'll probably see some scuba divers, as this is a favourite spot). Cross the sky-blue Johnson Street Bridge and follow Esquimalt Road for about 3 kilometres, then turn left onto Fraser Street and follow it down.

University of Victoria
Largely as the result of a few plant-collecting expeditions to China and Tibet mounted by Victoria horticulture buffs in the 1930s, UVic now has close to a hectare of rhododendron gar-

dens. With some plants as tall as 6 metres, and many unique to the area, this is easily one of the best rhododendron displays in the entire Pacific Northwest. (One of their gardeners works full-time keeping those beds in a state of exotic lushness.) Paths link the rhodos with a sequence of other gardens — shady bowers to sunny, poolside beds that can be admired while resting on ornate benches — that will keep flower fiends happily distracted for hours.

Uplands Park

Hidden in the middle of Oak Bay, just down from the posh Uplands estates, is one of the city's great treasures, a 30-hectare wild park. An attractive mix of forest and grassland that's been coloured with a generous scattering of wildflowers, Uplands Park has a criss-cross of trails that will keep strollers absorbed for a couple of hours. Access is easiest via Beach Drive; either park at the entrance to Cattle Point (a boat-launching area that is part of the park) or turn left on Dorset Road for two short blocks.

REGIONAL PARKS

Anyone seeking immersion in the diverse natural history of lower Vancouver Island just has to visit a few of the "wild" parks that are lovingly guarded by the Capital Regional District. From seashore to mountain top, from tiny nature sanctuaries to huge hiking expanses with prehistoric Indian rock carvings and incredible sea views, the CRD parks offer thousands of hectares of pleasure and fascination. (Two of these parks have nature houses and special park events like naturalist-led Sunday tidepooling or birdwatching expeditions. By dialing 474-7275 you can get a recorded message listing upcoming events and nature house hours.)

Albert Head Lagoon

Waterfowl, particularly mallards and mute swans, call this 7-hectare park home. The sheltered lagoon, with its pebbly shoreline, offers striking views of the Victoria skyline. This, along with Witty's and Devonian, are the three lagoon parks in Metchosin. Access is via the Old Island Highway to Sooke Road, then left onto Metchosin Road. After 4 kilometres, turn left at Farhill Road and left again at Park Drive.

Bear Hill

Connected to the Elk/Beaver Lake Park off the Pat Bay Highway, Bear Hill is a pleasant hike suitable for the family — it's about a half-hour to the top, and offers views of the Saanich Peninsula and Haro Strait. (See *Rural Rambles* in **Recreation**).

Coles Bay

This wooded parkland, a mix of deciduous and coniferous trees, boasts some Douglas firs that tower up to 30 metres. Down at knee level, the undergrowth includes such West Coast staples as salal, Oregon grape, and sword fern. It's a 10-minute hike down to Coles Bay, a protected cove on the Saanich Inlet that offers fairly warm swimming in summer. Access is via West Saanich Road: turn left on Ardmore Drive, then left again on Inverness Road.

East Sooke

Here's the big one, 1,400 hectares of wilderness park that pretty well sums up the southern West Coast environment. (See **Daytripping** for lots of info on the side trips and day-long hikes this mammoth Sooke park offers.)

Elk/Beaver Lake

This great spot offers the most "family fun" of any of the CRD parks: swimming, windsurfing, hiking, and canoeing are just part of what goes on here (see *In The Swim* in **Kidding Around**).

Francis/King

Named after two beloved local naturalists, this park has a special cedar boardwalk for the disabled and those with young ones still in strollers; its gentle slope offers easy access to one of Victoria's best nature preserves. Francis/King features 90 hectares of cedar and fir forests, thousands of wildflowers such as the calypso orchid, wetland areas with frogs and skunk cabbage, and flocks of cheerfully noisy birds. The park is a criss-cross of 10 varied and easily traversed trails, each one of which takes about a half-hour. The Nature House, open year-round, has informative displays on the area's flora and fauna. To check on nature programs and tours, call the CRD recorded-info line at 474-7275. Travel north on Douglas Street, turning left onto Burnside Road and following it till you reach Prospect Lake Road; follow it till you hit Munns Road, turn left, and the park entrance is less than a kilometre on your right.

Galloping Goose

When the defunct railroad out towards Sooke was scrapped, the CRD stepped in and has largely finished developing what will ultimately be a 58-kilometre "recreation corridor" along the old railbed. Named after the train engine that used to carry passengers as far as the now-abandoned goldmining centre of Leechtown, the Galloping Goose Corridor should be completely finished by 1998. But as of 1997, the 28-kilometre stretch from View Royal to Leechtown is open for hiking, mountain biking, and horse riding. Access begins near the Colwood Underpass, where you exit the highway and head west towards Sooke (a small parking lot is located on Atkins Road, just off Sooke Road).

Island View Beach

Here is one of Victoria's best beaches, complete with sand dunes and superb views out to the islands of Haro Strait. On a clear day, Washington State's Mount Baker looms high above Sidney, James, D'Arcy, and San Juan Islands. Sandbars create areas of shallow water that are great for beachcombers who want to snoop on the interesting intertidal life. Strollers who take the half-hour hike up to the north end of the beach where the grass-covered dunes are can admire the grebes, loons, and mallards. Access is via the Pat Bay Highway; turn right at Island View Road, which terminates in a parking area at the entrance to Island View.

Mill Hill

Spring is when this spot is in its glory: that's when a riot of wildflowers such as the chocolate lily and western buttercup adds perfume and colour to one of Victoria's most appealing rural retreats (it's no accident that the CRD has put its regional parks headquarters here!). The hike up the "summit trail" takes a half-hour, and the Saanich Peninsula sea views stretch between Mount Finlayson and Observatory Hill. Access is from the Trans-Canada Highway; turn left on Millstream Road, continue to the RCMP station, where you turn left onto Atkins Road and continue to the park entrance. Note: as of this writing, a trail is being developed connecting Mill Hill to Thetis Lake and Francis/King Park.

Mount Work

This is the outdoors equivalent of "one-stop shopping": after spending a brisk hour hiking to the 450-metre summit (the highest point on the Saanich Peninsula), you can go swimming, canoeing, or fishing in any of three lakes, or head down to McKenzie Bight and play Jacques Cousteau with the octopus and sea urchins there (see *Scuba Diving* in **Recreation**). Mount Work, located in the Highlands area of the Saanich Peninsula, is big enough to have two main entrances.

The Durrance Lake entrance is accessed via West Saanich Road: turn left on Wallace Drive and left again on Willis Point Road and go 4 kilometre; those wanting lake access should turn right at Durrance Close, while hikers should turn left on Ross-Durrance Road (look for the Gowland-Tod Provincial Park sign). The "summit trail" leads off from the gate at the entrance to the parking lot. To reach the less frequented Fork Lake entrance, take Burnside Road, turn right at Prospect Lake Road, then left on Munns Road, continuing along for just over 6 kilometres. Note: this park is poorly signed at present.

Roche Cove

With over 6 kilometres of forest trails (which wind through an ancient cedar grove), a hilltop lookout, and a secluded cove that's great for canoeing or kayaking, this 115-hectare park is a delight. It also connects with both the Galloping Goose Corridor (see above) and Matheson Lake Provincial Park, itself a superb recreation retreat. Access is via Colwood: follow the Sooke Road till you're about 27 kilometres out of town, then, just past 17-Mile House, turn left onto Gillespie Road and follow it for approximately another 3 kilometres.

Witty's Lagoon

Pretty well *everybody* in Victoria has come out and paid their respects to this beguiling park. Its mixture of woodlands, sandy beach, tidal lagoons, rocky shores, and a waterfall attract both flocks of visitors and flocks of visiting birds — blue herons, eagles, ospreys, and kingfishers are just some of the species that like to pass their days in this captivating sanctuary. The 5 kilometres of nature trails go through forest and out to a sandy spit popular with swimmers and picnickers.

Another section of the park is located off Olympic View

Drive. This detached and less-frequented Tower Point area of the park offers quiet views of the sandy spit and rocky shoreline. Aside from the chance to spot a harbour seal, cast a respectful glance at the nearby Haystock Islets, where the Coast Salish Indians used to bury their dead. And Witty's Nature House — located in a mobile trailer in the main parking lot — is open on weekends year-round, and for extended weekday hours during summer; drop in for park maps, brochures, nature displays, and a chat with the friendly staff.

Access is via the Old Island Highway to Sooke Road, then left onto Metchosin Road. After 6 kilometres you're at the main park entrance, on the left opposite the Metchosin Golf Club.

RECREATION

With the mildest climate in Canada and an unmatched setting for outdoors and sailing fanatics, it should be no surprise that sports and recreation are a pleasantly year-round obsession with most Victorians. And all those joggers, bikers, and Sundays- only rugby players are well aware of Victoria's tradition of amateur sports excellence, one that is out of all proportion to this area's small population. Many athletes — ranging from 1930s-era biking-to-basketball legend Doug Peden to the UVic-based rowers who have repeatedly struck Olympic gold — have inspired less talented but equally enthusiastic practitioners to make the most of this seductive Pacific playground.

BICYCLING

For everyone from Sunday cyclists to serious racers in those rainbow-coloured lycra skintights, Victoria's rolling hills and great vistas make for pure pedalling pleasure. It's not much fun biking downtown, so head for that scenery (and don't forget to pack a map!).

Start at Beacon Hill Park and follow Beach Drive along as far as you want; it's about 12 kilometres to Ten Mile Point/ Queenswood, where several pebbly pocket beaches make a great stopover to gobble that bagged lunch. (Look for "Public Beach Access" signs on the side roads.)

And consider dropping in on the nearby University of Victoria, with its country-club grounds and superb rhododendron gardens. If you have legs of iron, extend the Beach Drive route for several more kilometres: you'll get a diverting tour as you zig-zag through the grassy farmland areas of Central Saanich.

The municipality of Esquimalt has some great biking. Aside from attractive neighbourhoods in the Vic West area, there is a superb route along the scenic Gorge waterway. Ambitious riders should consider a jaunt out to the area's finest federal historic park, Fort Rodd Hill (a brisk hour from downtown; see **Sight-seeing**).

CANOEING/KAYAKING

Whether it's inland lakes or the wide-open ocean, the West Coast waters are a delight for anyone interested in paddle power. Independent-minded kayakers can pretty much jump off anywhere they want; some specific routes are suggested below.

Thetis Lake

This lake is popular as a casual day paddle, largely with canoeists. There are a couple of tiny islands that are a fun destination. Thetis is about 20 minutes out of the city, north along the Trans-Canada Highway (take the Colwood Exit onto Sooke Road, then turn right onto Six Mile Road).

Elk and Beaver Lakes

Canoeing doesn't get much more relaxed than at these connected lakes, 15 minutes out of town along the Pat Bay Highway.

The Gorge

Probably the most popular saltwater route for tourists is the hour-long paddle along the Gorge, a calm and scenic inland route that connects the Inner Harbour with Portage Inlet (but when the tide is going out it can be a bit rough under Tillicum Bridge). And if you rent from Ocean River Sports (see below), which is based next to the Harbour, the trip begins just past its doorstep.

Chatham/Discovery Islands

Paddlers who want a real ocean experience — but don't want to tangle with tough currents — should head towards these small and intriguing islands, just 3 kilometres offshore. Owned by the Songhees Indian Band and left alone like a wild park, Chatham and Discovery offer a good opportunity to spy on sea birds and curious seals. The easiest launch spot is Willows Beach in Oak Bay. Note: no trespassing.

The fishing in
Victoria waters is
truly spectacular

Sooke Basin

This one's good for beginners; a few offshore islands make a
nice destination. Take off from the northwest side of East Sooke
Park, at Anderson Cove — about a 50-minute drive from downtown.

Rentals

Ocean River Sports
1437 Store Street (Market Square)   *381-4233*

FISHING

B.C. is legendary for its salmon fishing. Chinook is the number
one trophy fish (the grandfathers can easily top 60 lbs on the
scale); coho, which are great scrappers and capable of acro-
batic displays when fighting the line, are the second-best catch
at up to 20 lbs. And in the last few years, halibut has begun to
rival salmon as the area's hottest fishery (halibut typically range
from 30 – 70 lbs, and can exceed 150 lbs!). Despite the much-
publicized "collapse" of the West Coast salmon fishery, only

certain areas connected to specific spawning grounds are affected. Victoria, thankfully, has been spared and sport fishing remains one of the greatest pleasures that awaits visitors to this area.

Charters

Unless you know a *lot* about fishing, it's best to go out with an experienced guide; aside from safety factors, salmon fishing is an art, and there's no substitute for the lifetime of local experience that a guide can provide. Chartering operations will also look after all the details like bait, tackle, licences, and which restrictions are currently in effect. All *you* have to do is work on feeling lucky. There are several charters that leave directly from downtown. The best ones are:

Adam's Fishing Charters
370-2326

A-1 Island Charters
479-7640

Harbour Charters
384-1224 (They do large groups of eight or more.)

Our best out-of-town individual chartering marinas are:

Cheanuh Marina
4901 East Sooke Road   *478-4880*

Oak Bay Marina
1327 Beach Drive   *598-3369*

Pacific Lions Marina
241 Becher Bay Road (Sooke)   *642-3816*

Pedder Bay
925 Pedder Bay Drive (Sooke)   *478-1771*

Tackle/Licences/Information

Although department stores like Eaton's and The Bay sell tackle, it's possibly best to hit the specialty sporting goods shops. The best all-round store downtown is **Robinson's**, 1307 Broad Street (385-3429). Also very good, and often a bit cheaper, is **Capital Iron**, 1900 Store Street (385-9703). **Jeune Bros & Peetz**, 570 Johnson Street (386-8778) has a good selection and knowledgeable staff.

Everyone, including children, *must* have the appropriate licence *on their person* while fishing. Licences are on sale where you buy your tackle. As well, don't forget to pick up a current copy of the government-issued regulations synopsis, which covers restrictions, limitations, and catch limits.

Where They Bite

Sooke
The area 40 kilometres southwest of Victoria offers the best fishing on the south Island. Anywhere from Becher Bay to Otter Point offers consistently prime conditions.

Victoria Waterfront
Whether you're casting from the Ogden Point breakwater or trolling off Dallas Road, the waters near downtown provide fine and convenient fishing.

Oak Bay
Beautiful and protected, with Chatham and Discovery islands to putt-putt around, the Oak Bay waters are a reliable year-round fishing locale.

Sidney
The fishing is always good in the waters off this small community, 24 kilometres north of Victoria on the Pat Bay Highway. The waters around Coal, Sidney, and James islands are good bets.

Brentwood Bay
You can't beat the scenery in Saanich Inlet and the fishing can be "hot" at certain times of the year (spring/early summer). On top of that these protected waters are fishable when other areas are too rough. Great area if you're looking for a family outing as well as a fishing trip.

Bamfield/Campbell River
These are two up-Island destinations that truly ardent fishermen might want to consider (although the angling around Victoria is darned fine). Bamfield, site of a famous marine research centre, is on the rugged west coast about four hours' drive from Victoria. Campbell River, about five hours' drive up the protected eastern side of Vancouver Island, is legendary for its fine fishing.

TENNIS

Beacon Hill Park

These three courts are right next to Beacon Hill Park's lawn bowling green. Drive up Cook Street towards the water, and park where May Street intersects on the left.

Cedar Hill Rec Centre
3220 Cedar Hill Road   *595-7121*

Four under-the-bubble courts, located at the corner of Finlayson Street and Cedar Hill Road (just behind Hillside Shopping Centre). Reserve the day before.

Oak Bay Rec Centre
1975 Bee Street   •   *595-7946*

Oak Bay Rec and its sister facility at Henderson Park (2291 Cedar Hill X Rd) have 13 outdoor and bubble courts between them. They also oversee five more courts at Carnarvon Park (take Fort Street out of town; just after it becomes Cadboro Bay Road, turn left onto Allenby Street). All that asphalt is on a reservation system, and it's best to phone the day before.

Stadacona Park

Five unreserved courts, in a pretty park halfway between downtown and Oak Bay Avenue near the intersection of Fort Street and Pandora Avenue. (The cross-street is Elford.)

GOLF

It's a 10-year wait on the membership lists for Victoria's best courses, but tourist drop-ins can head right for that first tee-off. From the spectacular views of the posh, ocean-bounded Victoria Golf Course to the public pitch 'n putt at Henderson Recreation Centre, the golfing greenery in this city is hard to beat.

Private Courses

Glen Meadows
1050 McTavish Road (Sidney)   *656-3921*

The area's longest course, Glen Meadows can challenge even a power hitter. Not much on drama or scenery. Green fees are $32; reserve the day before. Driving range available.

Gorge Vale
1005 Craigflower Road 386-3401

This demanding 18-holer is definitely a "golfer's" golf course. There are some great high-up tee shots and a variety of holes. A pretty course, and it's well maintained. Green fees are $48; reserve the day before.

Royal Colwood
629 Goldstream Avenue 478-8331

Closest to "tour" calibre of any of the area's facilities. Any serious golfer wanting to be challenged by water holes and dog's legs need take his cart no farther than this gorgeously maintained course. Green fees are $70; reserve after 11 AM the day before.

Uplands
3300 Cadboro Bay Road 592-1818

Here's a great "leisure" golfing romp. Uplands isn't long, and the course stays pretty level. A couple of water holes and numerous trees add technical challenge to this very attractive facility. Green fees are $70; reserve the day before.

Victoria
1110 Beach Drive 598-4322

At six in the morning, as the sun comes up over the San Juan Islands and the dew is still on the grass, this beautiful water-bounded course is golfer's heaven. The half-dozen holes on the ocean side are challenging because of the widely variable winds. All in all, a stunner. Green fees are $85 (and you *must* belong to a fellow club to merit reciprocal guest privileges); reserve the day before.

Public Courses

Ardmore
930 Ardmore Drive (Sidney) 656-4621

This fun nine-holer is for duffers who have outgrown the smaller par-three courses yet would be embarrassed about leaving a trail of divots behind on a premium facility. It's adequately maintained. Green fees are $16, or $24 for 18 holes; no reservations.

Cedar Hill
1400 Derby Road   595-3103

This is the only municipal course in town, and it is *busy*. It's not a long course, it's well maintained, and there are scenic views of the Olympic Mountains. Now if that sauntering four-some would only get on with it.... Green fees are $17; no reservations.

Cordova Bay
5333 Cordova Bay Road   658-4444

This is a fine intermediate-to-professional course, long and challenging. It's also elegantly landscaped, well maintained, and scenic. Green fees are $39.

Metchosin Golf & Country Club
4100 Metchosin Road   478-3266

Set in the rolling farmlands of Metchosin, this pretty nine-holer is a challenging par-three course. It is quiet and sweet out in the country (and the course is just across the road from Witty's Lagoon Beach, a superb site for picnicking and birdwatching). Green fees are $18 for 18 holes; reservations recommended.

Mount Douglas
4225 Blenkinsop Road   477-8314

This lush and green course is a *real* par-three facility; intermediate amateurs can try out their woods on some of the 240-yard holes. The stream towards the bottom of the course attracts not only stray balls but also a small armada of ducks. Lots of fun! Green fees are $7; no reservations.

Olympic View
643 Latoria Road (Metchosin)   474-3671

Serious golfers will love this challenging course, whose narrow fairways have been carved out of the forest. Scenery is gorgeous, the layout is spectacular, with enough up-and-down to give you a real workout. Green fees are $37; please reserve.

HIKING/WALKING

Victoria is a city of and for walkers. Whether it's a leaf-scuffing amble down the chestnut-lined boulevards of Fairfield or a lung-busting scramble up one of the nearby mountains, old-fashioned foot power can lead you to some of Victoria's most pleasurable experiences. The outlying areas contain a large number of wild areas, many of which have been declared parks and are under the protection of the Capital Regional District. Please remember that littering, camping, and fires are forbidden in these areas. (Refer also to **Gardens and Parks**.)

Urban Ambles

James Bay/Fisherman's Wharf

James Bay, which extends from around the Parliament Buildings down to Dallas Road and along to Beacon Hill Park, was the first part of the city to be domesticated as a burgeoning population looked beyond the wooden palisades of Fort Victoria for homes of their own. Many of the existing houses exhibit the ornate "gingerbread" detailing that was common until the 1920s. Stroll through the residential streets, heading towards Dallas Road, which affords spectacular sea views looking over the Strait of Juan de Fuca towards Washington State and the snow-capped Olympic Mountains. If you've already done the Beacon Hill tour, turn right and follow the water around to the west. One kilometre past the breakwater at Ogden Point you'll come across Fisherman's Wharf, a picturesque colony of trolling vessels and a few dozen rustic, handmade houseboats. There are usually a few characters selling crab or salmon right off of their boats. Or maybe just reward yourself with an ice cream cone from Barb's Fish and Chips, the city's only moored takeout restaurant.

Waterfront/Songhees/West Bay

Right in front of the Empress Hotel is the start of a superb hike for boat and water lovers. Begin at the Inner Harbour, walking below street level next to all those bobbing boats. Continue down Wharf Street and take the Johnson Street Bridge over towards Songhees, the new luxury-condo development. Hugging the shore is a sturdy footpath that continues for several kilometres; along with those blissful sea views and looks back at the Inner Harbour and Legislature, you'll come across jagged little bays where herons patiently stalk their lunch in the shallows, and the occasional parkland prominences that show off the distinct West Coast growths of Garry oak and arbutus trees. The walkway ends up at the West Bay Marina in Esquimalt (pay your respects to the resident Canada geese). A stroll there and back should take about two hours (unless you stop off for a restorative lager in Spinnakers Brew Pub, conveniently en route).

Rural Rambles

Bear Hill
It's an easy 30-minute hike up to the top of this hill, which cleverly avoided getting flattened as the glaciers retreated from the Saanich Peninsula 15,000 years ago. Bear Hill adjoins Elk/ Beaver Lake Park, and the damper soils at the base have grown a mantle of Douglas fir and salal bushes. These gradually give way to arbutus and Garry oak, which prefer drier slopes. Panoramic views from the top. Follow the Pat Bay Highway about 12 kilometres out of town. Turn left at Sayward Road, then right onto Brookleigh Road.

Mount Douglas/Mount Douglas Park
Mount Douglas offers a great panorama of Victoria and the surrounding waters. There are several little hikes off the car park near the top, and some people even like to scramble back all the way down without benefit of a trail. Just past the base of this 210-metre mountain is Mount Doug Park, with playing fields, swings, washrooms, and a woodsy trail that spills out onto a beach that offers an hour or more of beachcombing distractions. Follow Shelbourne Street till just before it connects up with the Cordova Bay section of Marine Drive.

Mount Finlayson
Right in Gowland-Todd Goldstream Provincial Park (where they have the autumn salmon spawning) stands Mount Finlayson, a steep 450-metre scramble that offers a hands-on climbing challenge to the recreational rambler. It takes less than an hour to get a gander at those super views from the peak. Goldstream is a half-hour's drive from town, north along the highway towards Duncan. Trail access is just off the parking lot.

SAILING/CRUISING

Victoria is a boater's paradise. With its mild climate, interesting geography, and a profusion of funky Gulf Islands, the area has enough hidden coves and popular destinations to keep marine explorers fascinated for months. There are simply too many chartering companies to include them all. A few of the more established ones are listed below.

Charters/Rentals

Bosun's Charters
2240 Harbour Road (Sidney)   656-6644

Offering mostly bareboat and some skippered charters, both sail and power; boats ranging from 8 metres to 12 metres. Three-day minimum.

Brentwood Inn Resort
7172 Brentwood Drive   652-2413

Aside from their party-plus 40-passenger yacht, these guys rent out power boats from 4 metres to 6 metres. Two-hour minimum.

Gulf Islands Cruising
2300 Canoe Cove Road (Sidney)   656-2628

Skippered or bareboat charters, half-day to weekly rentals, power and sailboats.

Pride of Victoria Cruises
1175 Beach Drive   598-4556

This 12-metre yacht specializes in 90-minute lunch cruises and three-hour evening outings, complete with elegant on-board dining (and some smashing sunsets). Sometimes they also do a "breakfast adventure cruise," with a scuba diver who brings up weird and wild stuff from underwater that makes a great show-and-tell for the kids. Also available for private charters.

Seahorse Sailing
2075A Tryon Road (Sidney)   655-4979

Mostly sailboat charters, with boats from 8 metres to 12 metres. Three-day minimum.

Routes/Destinations

Mariners with more time on their hands should plan a cruise that overnights at the sequence of marine parks dotting this area (moorage is free and there are no restrictions). The classic route is up Haro Strait about 16 kilometres to D'Arcy Island (this lovely anchorage used to be a leper colony, and eerie dreams have occasionally beset boaters with lively imaginations!). Continuing north, it's a shorter hop to Sidney Island, a favourite site with local boaters because its superb beaches are like those of a tropical lagoon. And if you have time, keep heading north to Portland Island: this little island is a paradise to hike on.

Sailors interested in hitting the major marine meccas should haul anchor and head towards the Gulf Islands. The two classic destinations are Bedwell Harbour on Pender Island (safe anchorage plus pub and hotel), and Galiano Island's equally well-equipped Montague Harbour.

Basically, Sidney, Bedwell, and Montague are the big triangle. Other places are more hazardous — due either to susceptibility to hostile weather conditions, or because of frankly hostile landowners who are very protective of their turf — and are best left for knowledgeable sailors. (The standard cruising bible for this area is Bill Wolferstan's *Cruising Guide to British Columbia, Vol. 1: The Gulf Islands*.)

SCUBA DIVING

The diving in the waters off Vancouver Island is considered some of the best in the world. Although the water lacks the underwater visibility of the tropics, this nutrient-rich marine environment feeds a profusion of life forms: everything from sea lions and sea urchins to a dozen different starfish and literally 400 species of fish live in B.C. waters. Note that many of the areas have strong tidal currents, and are for experienced divers only. Check for up-to-the-minute information from some of the dive shops listed below (and maybe sign on for a charter if you really want to get the most out of your underwater time).

Locations

Ogden Point

Head for the breakwater in James Bay, just five minutes from downtown. This marine park offers the easiest access to the pleasures of West Coast diving. Depths range from 6 metres to 21 metres, and offer everything from octopus and ling cod to colourful anemones.

Ten Mile Point
Just past Cadboro Bay Beach, Ten Mile Point offers particularly rich diving experiences because of the tremendous tidal currents that sweep by. There's an underwater wall just offshore that is carpeted with sea cucumbers, white anemones, abalone, and other filter feeders. Best access is via Seaview Road, Tudor Avenue, Baynes Road and onto the end of White Rock. Note: this is for experienced divers only (and carry a knife because of the kelp forests).

Saxe Point Park
Algae, sunflower stars, huge chitons, shrimp, gooseneck barnacles, and jellyfish are all on view at this fun dive. Go over the Johnson Street bridge onto Esquimalt Road for 3 kilometres, then turn left on Fraser Street and follow it to the park.

McKenzie Bight
A bit farther from town, on the Saanich Inlet, McKenzie Bight offers a protected inlet dive. Go down and take in all those exotic giant nudibranchs and other invertebrates plus a variety of fish. Travel on West Saanich Road, turning left on Wallace Drive and left again on Willis Point Road to Mark Lane, where you make a sharp left and continue along for 3 kilometres of rough road.

Rentals/Charters

All of the shops listed below rent equipment and can arrange charters. The waters around here can be cold; a quarter-inch neoprene suit is the *least* protection you'll want. And if you want air, better have proof of your diving certification.

Ocean Centre
800 Cloverdale Avenue   475-2202

Frank White's Scuba Shop
1855 Blanshard Street   385-4713

Sprocket Scuba Diving
2519 Douglas Street   361-3966

SWIMMING

If you're spurning the chlorinated waters of the various recreation centres, then grab your suit and head for the following
lakes and beaches.

Durrance Lake

Warmer than some of the lakes, and enough out of the way that
it's not *totally* overrun. There is a definite tendency for teens
with big hormones and even bigger ghetto blasters to destroy
the rural calm, however. Durrance Lake is accessed via West
Saanich Road: turn left on Wallace Drive and left again on
Durrance Road.

Elk/Beaver Lake

This is a super family area, with picnic facilities and woodsy
trails. Out along the Pat Bay Highway towards the ferries.

Thetis Lake

There's great swimming here and even an island that stronger
swimmers can head out to. There are several picnic areas and a
long trail — perfect for a pre-swim hike — that winds around
the lake. Thetis Lake Park is about 20 minutes from downtown,
north along the Trans-Canada Highway. Take the Colwood Exit
onto Sooke Road, then turn right onto Six Mile Road.

Prior Lake

People who like their swimming on the informal side might
want to head for this nude beach. Turn right, immediately past
the Island Highway underpass that leads out towards Colwood.
Keep going past a rifle range and then a small parking area for
Little Thetis (actually, many people go skinny-dipping here as
well). At the bottom of the hill you'll find another small parking area and a sign flagging Prior Lake.

Willows Beach

Ocean swimming isn't for everyone, but everyone seems to
show up at this attractive and sandy Oak Bay hangout … if
only to see what the latest bikini fashions are all about. Picnic
and washroom facilities make it fine for families.

DAYTRIPPING

Unless you're in Victoria for just a day or so, you should consider spending part of your time outside the city: enticing as our Quaintville is, some of the finest pleasures unique to the West Coast are to be had at remote beaches or in picturesque towns. And does it *really* matter that you'll be out of earshot of the silver bell summoning the faithful to tea at the Empress Hotel?

SAANICH PENINSULA

The largely rural Saanich Peninsula, due north of Victoria, has often been referred to in this guide; aside from Butchart Gardens, the area contains many of our best beaches, parks, and lakes. For a full day of leisurely sightseeing, maybe combine Butchart, some beachcombing, and a park visit. (Get some ideas from the *Regional Parks* section of **Gardens and Parks**; look for Coles Bay, Island View Beach, and Mount Work.)

Sidney

Sidney, boasting a population of approximately 11,000, is located on the east side of the Saanich Peninsula, about 27 kilometres north of Victoria. It is the business hub of the largely rural peninsula, with two official ports of entry to Vancouver Island close at hand: the Anacortes Ferry coming up from the United States and the Victoria International Airport.

This seaside town is small and pretty, and it faces Haro Strait with its picturesque islands and magnificent sea views. There are several marinas nearby, with easy access to excellent sailing and fishing. It is also the main shopping centre for the peninsula, with a delightful small-town atmosphere.

Log birling is one of
the highlights of All-
Sooke Day
(*Tourism BC*)

Sidney Island

This tiny island, a provincial park just 10 minutes by ferry
from Sidney, is a family-oriented gem. The ferry drops you off
at a long, narrow sandy spit where the water gets warm enough
for swimming (and the snorkelling and diving are excellent).
When you're tired of swimming or sunbathing, hike around
through the woodsy trails and rolling farmland, looking for the
deer and the exotic birds that were transplanted here (the dock-
ing area is well signed with naturalist info). The area is also
great for crabbing and shrimping, so maybe have an authentic
West Coast feast on the picnic tables. Overnight camping is
allowed. Access is via the "The Little Ferry," which leaves from
the government wharf at the end of Beacon Avenue. Ferry season is from May through to November; sailings fluctuate, but
are every two hours in summer.

Sooke

Far west from Victoria lies the pleasant village of Sooke, which
was first settled in 1849. Access is via Sooke Road (a.k.a. Highway 14); it's about an hour's drive, so consider dropping in at
17 Mile House, a historic roadhouse pub.

Long past its short-lived glory days during the Leechtown
gold rush of the 1860s, Sooke now pays tribute to its pioneer
past in the interesting Sooke Region Museum, which includes
historical artifacts, photographs, scale models, and a tour of
the restored nineteenth-century "Moss Cottage" (just off the

highway at the entrance to Sooke).

Gorgeous Sooke Harbour is the gateway to some of the world's best salmon fishing, but beach bums will want to push a bit farther along to investigate some of the West Coast's most unspoiled beaches. First up is pebbly and pleasing French Beach Provincial Park, with campsites and fine views (about 20 kilometres past Sooke). If you're starting to feel peckish, stop in at famed Point No Point; after a hike down along those beach trails, let their restaurant fill you up with high tea or some tasty sandwiches.

The next big stop is Jordan River, which is a surfer's mecca (33 kilometres past Sooke). And just past Jordan River is the ever-popular China Beach: this surf-washed beach, with those big Pacific waves rolling in and crashing onshore, pretty much defines the ocean experience. It's another 20 kilometres to classy Sombrio Beach, which gives another strong taste of the wide-open Pacific Ocean (some pretty brutal logging has taken the pristine bloom off the place, but the *beach* is still amazing). It's a bit of a hike down from the parking lot, so you know the beach won't be crowded out by the RV set. And if you've come this far, keep on going to Port Renfrew, which boasts the amazing tidepools at Botanical Beach (see **Ecotourism**).

East Sooke Park

This mammoth park is 1,400 hectares of West Coast wilderness: jagged seacoast, 270-metre mountain tops, abandoned mine sites, and a complete range of plant, bird, and animal life. Definitely better for hiking boots instead of open-toed sandals, the dozen trails that criss-cross East Sooke Park range from half-hour jaunts up to a seven-hour marathon that begins at Aylard Farm, follows the rugged coastline along to Iron Mine Bay, then cuts north to the protected beauties of Anderson Cove (and you'd better have a second vehicle waiting there, if you don't want to retrace your steps!). Many visitors will happily content themselves with a visit to the famed petroglyphs (Indian rock carvings), followed by a second leg down to the viewpoint at Beechey Head. This hike, which begins at Aylard Farm, is about three hours there and back (note the small and beautiful pocket beaches adjacent to the Aylard Farm area).

Access to East Sooke Park is via the Old Island Highway; turn onto Sooke Road, then left onto Happy Valley Road to

The gigantic outdoor murals at Chemainus turned a dying milltown into a brilliant tourist attraction (*Lorene J. Green*)

Rocky Point Road. Follow Rocky Point till you reach East Sooke Road, which leads to the three major park entrances at Aylard Farm (turn again onto Becher Bay Road), Anderson Cove, and Pike Road (which leads to the superb viewpoint at Pike Point). More intrepid hikers are advised to get a map of the park by dropping into the info centre at the Sooke Museum (just off the highway as you're coming into Sooke). Allow about an hour's driving time from Victoria.

UP-ISLAND

Chemainus
Known nationally as "The Little Town That Did," Chemainus refused to become a ghost town when the Macmillan-Bloedel sawmill pulled the plug in 1983. Instead, Chemainus artists grabbed pots of paint and started daubing larger-than-life murals on many of the town's public walls. These 30 colourful depictions of the local history are truly inspiring.

For $1 you can buy the handy walking-tour map, with all the sites keyed in (during summer these are available from either the Society kiosk or from the Tourist Info Centre; in the off-season, try Pharmasave or Chemainus Book & Card). These award-winning murals are accessed via the Trans-Canada Highway. About an hour's drive north of Victoria you should turn right onto Henry Road (take your cue from the green highway signs), turn left just past the Mount Brenton golf course, then follow Chemainus Road right into downtown. Info: 246-3944.

Cathedral Grove

If ever a grove of trees deserved to be called a cathedral, it's this stand of ancient and towering Douglas firs, which should harken to the druid in everyone. The Forest Service is wont to get all sentimental and refer to trees this inspiring as "mighty monarchs of the forest" (that is, when they're not giving permission to the logging companies to do a slash-and-burn in our old-growth stands), and even a quick stroll through the trails of this 120-hectare site should give you some understanding of why B.C.'s "tree-hugging" environmentalists get so confrontational when yet another of the vanishing stands of magnificent timber is threatened with ecological devastation. Cathedral Grove is located about 32 kilometres west of Parksville, on Highway 4.

GULF ISLANDS

When big-city folk from Central Canada make jealous jokes about "West Coast flakes," they are often doing a clumsy job of describing the unique lifestyle on our Gulf Islands. This archipelago consists of more than 300 islands scattered throughout the protected waters on the lee of Vancouver Island. Home to artists, sheep herders, writers, retirees, musicians, potters, and thousands of other folk who would rather wear gumboots than Gucci loafers, the pastoral Gulf Islands offer a soul-restoring retreat from the urban din.

The largest islands are the ones to visit. Most visitors will want to have a car, but the bicycling is pretty good here, if a bit steep (but please respect the narrow roads and ride prudently). These islands are great for hiking, swimming, boating, fishing, and just general relaxing. And people who can't resist shopping on vacation will find these islands are home to some of the province's finest potters and other artisans. Ferries leave frequently from the Swartz Bay Terminal at the north end of the Pat Bay Highway, about 30 minutes' drive from downtown. Maps on the Gulf Islands are available from the Tourism Vic-

toria tower in the Inner Harbour. Phone 386-3431 for current
schedule information.

Salt Spring Island

This is the most populous of the Gulf Islands. The ferry lands
at Fulford Harbour, a little speck of a place that is at its best
when you're devouring a huge chocolate ice cream cone and
waiting for your return ferry. Head towards Ganges, which is
the commercial centre of the island. Even though it has become a tad overdeveloped (even islanders want to rent Tom
Cruise videos), this town makes for a diverting visit — tour
either the waterfront or the bustling Saturday-morning farmers' market that sets up in front of the park (and if you are
hungry, Moby's, the nearby marine pub, has great food). Destinations worth visiting include the top of Mount Maxwell,
just a short drive away (make sure your car is up to the bounc-
ing trip up an unpaved road), and Ruckle Park, on the south-
east corner of the island. This gorgeous provincial park is a
super place to have your picnic with a seaview backdrop (on
Beaver Point Road, off the Fulford-Ganges Road).

North and South Pender Islands

This is two islands for the price of one: North and South Pender
are connected by a narrow, single-lane bridge. This hilly island
offers many pretty sea views as its roads twist and turn. There
are tennis courts at the community centre, just before you leave
North Pender via the bridge. Beachcombers should cross the
bridge to South Pender and take the short gravel access road to
Mortimer Spit, which is a fine place to bask in the sun or watch
for shorebirds or eagles wheeling in the sky.

Bedwell Harbour on South Pender is one of the two big
sailing destinations in all the Gulf Islands. There is a good pub
here, and a deli and other shops. But if you're not into nautical
hobnobbing, you may prefer the funkier pub located at the less
tony Port Browning Marina on the north island (great burgers,
too!). The ferry lands at the dock at Otter Bay on North Pender.

Mayne Island

Mayne is one of the less travelled islands, and the better for it.
Its rolling orchard lands and numerous flocks of sheep lend it
a rustic flavour and gentle ambience that can soothe even the
most stressed-out visitor. From the ferry terminal at Village

Bay, drive along Village Bay Road to Miner's Bay. After a hike up Mount Parke, seek out a fine, warm-water splash in pretty Bennett Bay (head east from Miner's Bay till you reach the end of Fernhill Road, go left onto Wilks Road and then make a quick right). Shoppers hoping to pick up some handweaving or a pottery set have come to the right place: many excellent artisans have dotted their shops around this tiny island. Want either a sweet nibble or a stomach-filling brioche stuffed with ham, spinach, and cheese? Head for the frequently full Robert's Chocolates on Fernhill Road.

KIDDING AROUND

Let's face it, not *all* of Victoria's attractions and amenities are going to keep your children entranced. If their eyes are glazing over as you pull up to the umpteenth historical site, or you've spent too long shopping for sensible woollen clothes and those tugs on the end of your arm are getting truly desperate, it's time to let loose and enjoy Victoria from a kid's perspective. Heck, you might even find that beachcombing off Dallas Road or floating through Butterfly World become some of the most treasured mental snapshots of your vacation.

Following are a range of activities and visits that include both physical fun and exercise for the imagination. Although there are a few touristy recommendations, the emphasis is on no-cost options that we locals use to keep our young ones happily distracted. Make sure you've got a map (good ones are available free from Tourism Victoria in the Inner Harbour), as Victoria streets tend to twist, turn, and change name without rational explanation.

IN THE SWIM

For freshwater fun, there are many lakes to choose from. The adjoining Elk and Beaver lakes are about 15 minutes' drive from town (Beaver is particularly family oriented, as it's the only lake in the region that has lifeguards). Follow Blanshard Street north till it becomes the Pat Bay Highway; the turnoff for Beaver Lake is left on Haliburton Road, while Elk Lake is a bit farther along at Sayward Road. Thetis Lake is a similar distance from downtown, only it's accessed off the Trans-Canada Highway leading up-Island (take the Colwood Exit onto Sooke Road, then turn right onto Six Mile Road). All three lakes are set in parks, complete with picnic tables, hiking trails, and other amenities.

Beach bums should start with either Cadboro Bay or Willows, as both beaches are sandy and clean, with well-maintained washroom facilities. Cadboro Bay Beach is located near the University of Victoria; just turn right at the four-way stop where Cadboro Bay Road meets Sinclair Road. Willows Beach is in Oak Bay; use Beach Drive and savour those pretty sea views en route.

Those seeking slightly more adventurous ambles, with pebbled beaches, tidepools, and a jumble of driftwood to clamber over should consider Dallas Road (just adjoining Beacon Hill Park), or Mount Douglas Park and Cordova Bay (slightly farther north along Beach Drive).

If it's cool out (or you just like the taste of chlorine), head for the Commonwealth Pool (4636 Elk Lake Drive, 727-7108), which was built in 1994 as the aquatic centre for the Commonwealth Games and is a national-calibre facility. Aside from two 50-metre pools, it also boasts Victoria's only wave pool; a *huge* slide, diving towers, family change rooms, weight room, and a gym round out the offerings. (And there's even a regional library here so you can exercise your mind as well as your body!) To get there travel out Blanshard Street (which becomes the Pat Bay Highway); look for the Royal Oak Drive exit, turn left on Royal Oak (at the overpass), then right at the first set of lights.

There are two other pool options: the Crystal Pool (2275 Quadra Street, 383-2522), or the Oak Bay Rec Centre (1975 Bee Street, 595-7946); both have regular pools and wading pools for pre-aquatic tots. The Crystal is closer to downtown, but it can't compete with Oak Bay Rec, which boasts a 45-metre slide, Tarzan swing, weights, ping-pong, skating, and skateboarding during the summer (they installed a "half-pipe" so daredevils can do those gravity-defying stunts).

And if you're prepared to make a day of it, head up the Old Island Highway past Sooke in search of the miniature marvels contained in the tidepools at Botanical Beach (see **Ecotourism**).

PLAYGROUNDS/VISITS

Beacon Hill just *has* to be one of the best playgrounds, any-where. Its 75 hectares contain splendidly manicured gardens, rustic stone bridges, flocks of ducks waiting to be fed, and cricket pitches where folks in white play that incomprehensi-ble game. Best of all, it has a petting zoo, where children get to be hands-on with a menagerie of friendly barnyard folk (in-cluding rabbits, baby goats, and miniature horses). And after feeding the ducks and visiting the petting zoo, make it a triple-header by visiting the kids' water park. There are also picnic tables, but if you don't have a basket just head over towards the Beacon Drive-in (across Douglas Street near the southwest corner of the park) and invest in a round of soft ice cream cones.

Don't overlook **MacDonald Park**, which is just a few blocks behind the Parliament Buildings in James Bay (corner of Oswego and Simcoe streets). Here your kids can get happy with swings, slides, hand-over-hand climbing, plus a palisaded, semi-underground fort that comes equipped with an ingenious "tunnel." The park adjoins a massive grass playing field that is several frisbee tosses wide.

Cadboro-Gyro Park (which adjoins Cadboro Bay Beach) is a great combo of grass and sand. If you've already taken a low-tide hike (were you lucky enough to find a weathered In-dian arrowhead lying in the sand?), let those youngsters loose above the high-tide line on a great lineup of fantasy fun which includes a huge concrete octopus, a leaping salmon (whose open mouth is typically "devouring" a couple of grinning kids), and 30 sinuous metres of "Caddie" — a harmless, and very photogenic, replica of the horrible sea serpent that's supposed to inhabit the nearby waters.

The **Swan Lake Christmas Hill Nature Sanctuary** is a very special 50-hectare park that will appeal to kids of all ages. There's a floating boardwalk and also a trail that rings both the lake and marshlands of this protected site, giving great views of the numerous resident and transient birds: depending on the time of year, this birdwatcher's paradise attracts numerous spe-cies of wild ducks, geese, blue herons, cormorants, eagles, and owls (and river otters and muskrats sometimes put in an ap-pearance). The Nature House has various exhibits and appealing hands-on displays that will engage all your senses. Particularly popular are the lake-life aquariums and a micro-zoo starring a western painted turtle, a demonstration beehive, and some slithery garter snakes. Follow Blanshard Street north out of town; take the McKenzie Street exit, turn right onto Rainbow Street, and follow the sign to the parking lot. The Sanctuary is open during weekdays from 8:30 AM to 4 PM; weekends and holidays the hours are noon – 4 PM (479-0211).

And the **Inner Harbour Causeway** is worth a visit. Aside from the artists (several of whom will sketch a quick cartoon of you or your family), there are many talented buskers competing for your attention … and spare change. And after you've taken in all the Andean flute music, jazz, folk, and C&W tunes, check out the boats and watch for seals and other harbour-based wildlife.

KID-SIZED ATTRACTIONS

The following attractions are particularly good bets to intrigue young folk (for complete descriptions, please refer to the **Sightseeing** chapter of this guide): Miniature World, Butterfly World, Undersea Gardens, Crystal Garden, Royal B.C. Museum, and Fort Rodd Hill. And if you and your children have divergent interests, then consider dropping them off at Oak Bay Recreation's "Skidaddle Camp," which combines both indoor activities such as computers, in-line skating, games, arts and crafts with outdoor sports and other fun. Cost is $22.50 for an 8 AM – 5 PM day, Monday-Friday. Oak Bay Rec is at 1975 Bee Street (595-7946).

BIBLIOGRAPHY

Visitors interested in reading more about this corner of the Pacific Northwest might want to seek out some of the titles listed below.

A Dream of Islands, Philip Teece (Orca)
Flavours of Victoria, Andrea and David Spalding (Orca)
Hiking Trails I, (Victoria Trails Information Society)
Hiking Trails II, (Victoria Trails Information Society)
Hiking Trails III, (Victoria Trails Information Society)
Island Cycling, David Payne (Orca)
Island Paddling, Mary Ann Snowden (Orca)
Island Pubbing II, Robert Moyes (Orca)
Pass the Bottle, Eric Newsome (Orca)
Rumrunner — The Life and Times of Johnny Schnarr,
    Marion Parker/Robert Tyrrell (Orca)
Victoria — Another View, Robert Amos (Orca)